Roman
Myths

Acknowledgements

The author wishes to thank in particular Dr Susan Walker of the British Museum Department of Greek and Roman Antiquities, and Dr Dora Thornton of the Department of Medieval and Later Antiquities, for bibliographical and other help in selecting items from the British Museum collections for the illustrations.

Picture credits

Abbreviations: BM = By courtesy of the Trustees of the British Museum
BMCRR = *Coins of the Roman Republic in the British Museum* (1910)
BMCRE = *Coins of the Roman Empire in the British Museum*, I, (1923)
PCR = *Principal Coins of the Romans*, I (1978)

Front cover BM GR 1927.12–12.1; pp. 4–5 BM PD Oo.7.149.H.308; p. 6 Serge Ransford; p. 9 BM *BMCRR* (Rome) 3891; p. 10 BM CM 1931-5-4-29, *PCR* 23; p. 11 BM GR Bronze 1523; p. 12 (top) BM GR 1946.4–23.1; (below) By courtesy of the Allard Pierson Museum, Amsterdam, 1606; p. 15 BM GR Terracotta D 690; p. 17 BM CM *BMCRR* (East) 31; p. 18 The Ny Carlsberg Glyptotek, Copenhagen, 494a; p. 19 BM PD Oo.8.269.H.303; p.21 BM CM *BMCRE* I (Tiberius) 16; p. 22 BM PD Oo.7.240.H.310; p. 25 Römisch-Germanisches Museum, Köln, Inv. 70.3; p. 28 BM MLA 66, 12–29, 21; p. 30 BM GR 1902.1–16.1, Silver 73; p. 32 BM CM *BMCRR* (Rome) 926; p. 33 BM GR 1840.1–11.15, BM Cat. Vases H.1; p. 34 BM CM *BMCRR* (Rome) 2322; p. 35 Musée du Louvre, no. 188, photo Réunion des musées nationaux, Paris; p. 37 BM CM *BMCRE* (Augustus) 76; p. 42 BM GR 1983.12–29.1; p. 44 Musée du Louvre, no. 189, photo Réunion des musées nationaux, Paris; p. 47 BM MLA 1878, 12–30, 408; p. 50 BM MLA 1855, 12–1, 74; p. 54 BM CM *BMCRE* I (Augustus) 30; p. 56 (top left) BM CM *BMCRR* (Rome) 3652; (right) BM GR 1979. 11–8.1; p. 60 BM PD 1868.8–22.38; p. 64 BM GR Sculpture 2310, Towneley Collection; p. 67 BM GR 1925.12–18.1, Sculpture D 69; p. 69 (top right) Drawing of BM GR Bronze 633; (lower left) BM GR 1772–3–2.26, Bronze 604; p. 70 (top right) BM GR Bronze 1574; (below) BM GR 1893.5–1.6, Silver 136; p. 72 BM GR 1899.2–18.46; p. 73 BM GR 1873.2–8.1, Painting 24; p. 74 BM PRB OA 248; p. 77 BM CM *BMCRR* (Rome) 3415; p. 78 BM PD 1947.1–10.1; chapter openers Sue Bird.

THE · LEGENDARY · PAST

Roman
Myths

JANE F. GARDNER

Published for the
Trustees of the British Museum by
BRITISH MUSEUM PRESS

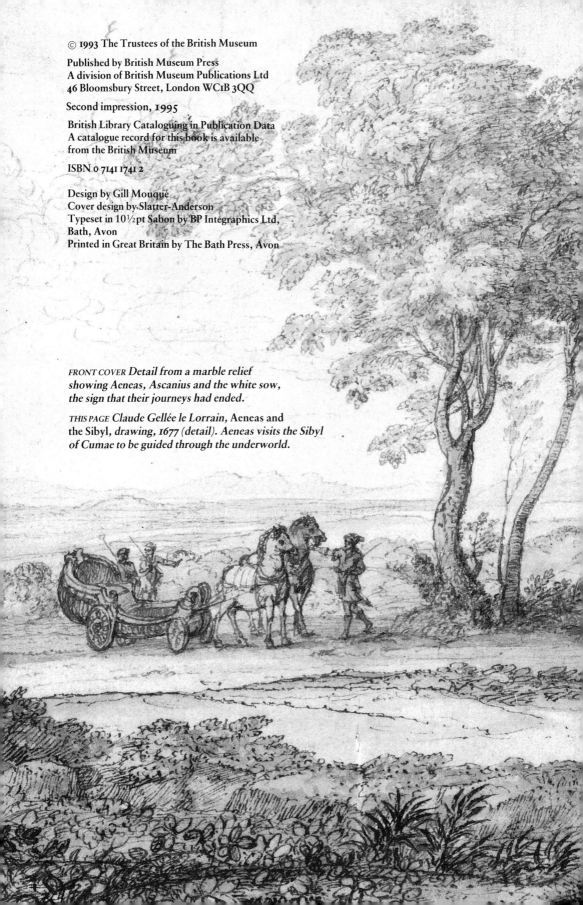

Published by British Museum Press
A division of British Museum Publications Ltd
46 Bloomsbury Street, London WC1B 3QQ

Second impression, 1995

British Library Cataloguing in Publication Data
A catalogue record for this book is available
from the British Museum

ISBN 0 7141 1741 2

Design by Gill Mouqué
Cover design by Slatter-Anderson
Typeset in 10½pt Sabon by BP Integraphics Ltd,
Bath, Avon
Printed in Great Britain by The Bath Press, Avon

FRONT COVER *Detail from a marble relief
showing Aeneas, Ascanius and the white sow,
the sign that their journeys had ended.*

THIS PAGE *Claude Gellée le Lorrain,* Aeneas and
the Sibyl, *drawing, 1677 (detail). Aeneas visits the Sibyl
of Cumae to be guided through the underworld.*

Contents

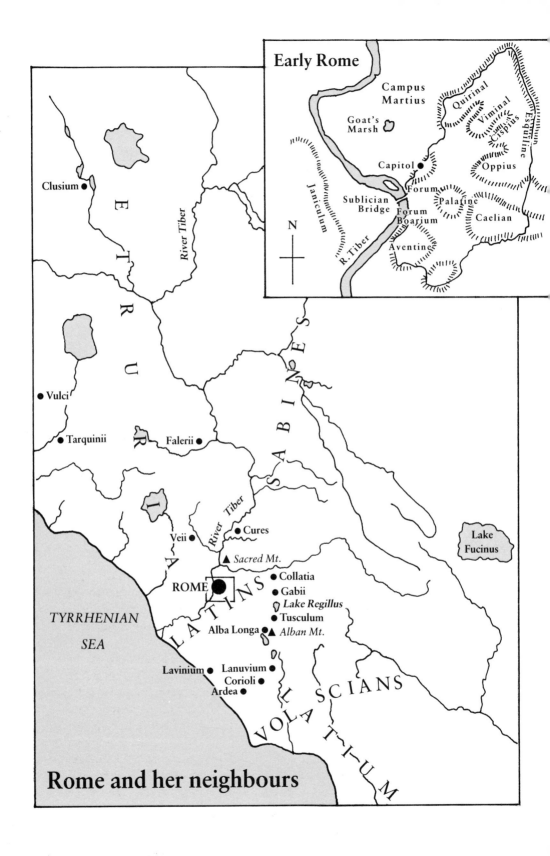

Early Rome

Campus Martius

Goat's Marsh

Quirinal

Viminal

Cispius

Esquiline

Capitol

Forum

Oppius

Janiculum

Sublician Bridge

Forum Boarium

Palatine

Caelian

R. Tiber

Aventine

N

E T R U R I A

Clusium

River Tiber

S A B I N E S

Vulci

Tarquinii

Falerii

Lake Fucinus

Veii

River Tiber

Cures

Sacred Mt.

ROME

Collatia

Gabii

Lake Regillus

Tusculum

Alba Longa

Alban Mt.

TYRRHENIAN SEA

L A T I N S

Lavinium

Lanuvium

Corioli

Ardea

V O L S C I A N S

L A T I U M

Rome and her neighbours

Introduction

T he Romans, it has been said, had no myths, only legends. The *Oxford
English Dictionary* describes myth as 'fictitious narrative usually involving supernatural persons, actions, or events, and embodying some
popular idea concerning natural or historical phenomena'. Most Roman myths
do not fit this definition at all well. They are presented in ancient writers not as
fiction, but as the early history of the Roman people – even though we can
observe their content changing before our very eyes. Many myths do not involve
the gods at all, or only to a small extent, and these are not myths *about* the
Roman gods themselves.

In the first century BC a speaker in Cicero's philosophical dialogue *On the
Nature of the Gods* distinguishes between mythological stories about the gods,
which he regards as something Greek, and Roman expectations of religion;
Roman religion is made up of (1) ritual, (2) taking auspices, and (3) prophetic
warnings issued by interpreters of Sibylline oracles, or of the entrails of sacrificed animals, on the basis of portents and omens. 'I am quite certain that
Romulus by instituting auspices, and Numa ritual, laid the foundations of our
state, which would never have been able to be so great had not the immortal
gods been placated to the utmost extent.'

In other words, *stories* about the gods were unimportant; religion's function was to maintain a stable relationship between the gods and the state, and
Rome's past success was its justification. A generation later a Greek writer,
Dionysius of Halicarnassus, spoke approvingly of Rome's lack of myths (especially of the morally discreditable kind) about the gods. This he ascribes to the
foresight of Romulus, who saw that what was paramount was maintaining the
favour of the gods, through suitable ritual practice, and the encouragement of
civic virtues.

Two other factors that certainly play a part in determining the character of
Roman myth are, firstly, the ancient view, common both to Greeks and to
Romans, of what history was for and how it should be written, and, secondly,
the fact that the earliest detailed accounts available to us come in writers from
the first centuries BC and AD. By that time Rome had already developed into a
highly sophisticated, urban society, whose culture, literature and thought were
deeply permeated by centuries of influence from Greek literature and culture;
the 'myths' are preserved in writings that are the product of highly refined and
self-conscious literary techniques. Authors felt free to reshape and even make
additions to the traditional stories.

Our main sources

Livy (c. 59 BC–AD 17) wrote a history of Rome in 142 books, from the foundation of Rome to 9 BC. Book 1, after briefly outlining the events from Aeneas' departure from Troy to the birth of Romulus and Remus, contains the story of the foundation of Rome and the reigns of its seven kings. Book 2 deals with the establishment of the Roman Republic and its earliest struggles.

The greatest work of **Virgil** (70–19 BC) was the *Aeneid*, an epic poem in twelve books, recounting the adventures of Aeneas after his departure from Troy until his arrival in Italy and the union of Trojans and Italians. There are several prophetic looks ahead to the future greatness of Rome, culminating in the destined appearance of the emperor Augustus (whose family claimed descent from Aeneas' divine mother, Venus).

Ovid (43 BC–AD 17 / 18) makes occasional use of Roman myth in several of his published poetical works. One, the *Fasti*, was an account of the Roman calendar, month by month, including descriptions and purported explanations of the origins of the sacred rites and festivals of the Roman religious year. Unfortunately only the first six books, January to June, survive. *Metamorphoses* includes some Roman tales, culminating in the deification of Julius Caesar, and ends with an encomium of Augustus.

Dionysius of Halicarnassus came to Rome as a teacher of rhetoric at about the time of Augustus Caesar's achieving sole leadership (30 / 29 BC) and stayed there for twenty-two years. He wrote *Roman Antiquities*, a romantic and rhetorical history of Rome from earliest times to the beginning of the first Punic War (264 BC). It was a panegyric of early Rome, aimed at reconciling Greeks to being ruled by Romans.

Ancient Latin scholarship also preserved some information, even although in abbreviated and often scrappy form. Marcus Terentius **Varro** (116–27 BC) devoted twenty years after his retirement from public life to research and writing, and he had a prodigious output. A later writer credited him with having edited 490 books by the time he was seventy-seven. Among his lost works was *Divine and Human Antiquities*, in forty-one books. Besides a treatise on agriculture, all of his work that survives is about a quarter of *The Latin Language*, which contains many antiquarian snippets. We also have part of the epitome by Sextus Pompeius **Festus** (second century AD) of a similar work by a learned freedman, Verrius Flaccus, the teacher of Augustus' grandsons.

Plutarch (c. AD 46–after 120), a Greek who travelled widely in the Roman world on public business, was also prolific. His best known work is the *Parallel Lives of Greeks and Romans*, of which twenty-two pairs and four separate biographies survive. For early Rome, we have his *Lives* of the kings Romulus and Numa, of Publius Valerius Publicola, one of the first consuls, and of Coriolanus. His *Roman Questions* discusses Roman customs and religious rituals.

None of these works is earlier than the first century BC, that is seven centuries after the traditional date of the foundation of Rome. What sources did these writers have?

A coin issued by the Roman moneyer L. Marcius Philippus in 55 BC: on one side, king Ancus Marcius, legendary builder of Rome's first aqueduct, on the other the Aqua Marcia (144 BC), with the equestrian statue of its builder Q. Marcius Rex.

Mainly they relied on earlier writers. The first known Roman historian (of whom only a few fragments survive) was Quintus Fabius Pictor, who wrote, at the end of the third century BC, a history of Rome from the origins to the middle of the third century. Like Rome's earliest known poets, he wrote in Greek; the first to write a historical account in Latin was the elder Cato, half a century later. Later writers, such as Livy, based their accounts, not on original research (for which there were virtually no materials) but on those of their predecessors, sometimes consciously trying to assess the value of conflicting versions, but more often than not picking the one that made the best story or the most suitable for their particular purposes. The two things that were of main importance for most ancient writers of history were the literary quality of the work, and its didactic value. 'What makes the study of history particularly beneficial and profitable,' wrote Livy, 'is that you have lessons from all manner of experience set out in full view as if on a memorial, and from there you may choose both for yourself and for your country examples of what to imitate and what things (bad begun and worse ended) to avoid.' This meant, amongst other things, that writers would interpret the past in terms of the issues of their own time.

The period from the supposed origins of Rome down to the end of the monarchy and establishment of the Republic (traditionally 509 BC) cannot be called 'historical' in our sense of the word; neither can much of what appears in literary accounts of the first generation or two of the Republic. Modern scholars argue about whether any historical truth can be said to exist at all in the stories about the period of the kings (and if there is, how to identify it), and the traditional accounts of the early days of the Republic are also agreed to be full of invention and contamination from later sources. For anyone interested in myth-making, however, these traditions are a treasure-house, for in them, and in the way they change and develop right down through the historical period, we see the Romans defining themselves through the stories they tell about their past – that is, through their 'myths'. They use a variety of materials, such as ideas and motifs copied from Greek mythology and history, motifs of a traditional 'folk-tale' type, and stories from the family traditions of some of the great Roman families. Republican moneyers issued coin types referring to their supposed ancestors in the legendary past. Historians disseminated the family traditions;

9

the prominence of the Fabii, the Valerii and the Claudii in the history of the early Republic probably owes something to Fabius Pictor, and to Valerius Antias and Claudius Quadrigarius, who wrote their own histories of Rome round about 80 BC.

These family legends appealed particularly to historical writers and also to orators like Cicero (even though they might sometimes express scepticism about them) because of their value as what the Romans called *exempla*, illustrations of a particular moral truth ('what to imitate and what things to avoid'). The early books of Livy, like the historical 'flash-forwards' in Virgil, have many of these patriotic legends exemplifying the 'Roman' virtues.

The Romans, like the Greeks, were also particularly interested in aetiology, i.e. accounting for beginnings, the beginning of rituals, of place-names, of institutions, of cities, of the whole Roman people and its history. This does not mean that they wanted actually to find out how they began, simply to tell a satisfactory story about them.

So, for instance, the beginnings of the main political religious and civic institutions of historical Rome are allocated among the seven kings (themselves mainly imaginary): Romulus – the senate, the 'curiate' assembly and the 'centuries' of cavalry; Numa – the calendar and the major priesthoods; Hostilius – treason trials, and religious procedures for making peace; Ancus Marcius – procedures for declaring war, Rome's first prison, bridge and aqueduct; Tarquinius Priscus ('the First') – the first stone wall round the city, the annual Roman games; Servius Tullius – the census, the tribal system and the hierarchical 'centuriate' assembly. Even the main sewer was attributed to a king, Tarquinius Superbus ('the Proud'), though the parts of it that survive go back no earlier than the fourth century BC.

Roman gods and Greek myths

The Romans, it seems, had a native god, or gods, for almost every important object or activity. For instance, Consus ('storage' – though Varro thought the name came from 'counsel'), Pales (goddess of flocks and herds) and Robigo / –us (blight) were agricultural; Janus looked after doorways, Faunus was the god of wild things, Silvanus the god of woodlands and untilled land; and there were

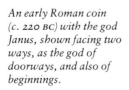

An early Roman coin (c. 220 BC) with the god Janus, shown facing two ways, as the god of doorways, and also of beginnings.

The woodland god Silvanus, wearing an animal skin and bearing a tree in one hand; the other originally held something, perhaps a pruning-hook.

In the early Empire freedman families liked to be portrayed on their tombs in the guise of gods. From the neck down, this young woman is Venus; her hairstyle closely resembles that worn by Hadrian's mother-in-law.

Terracotta lamp showing the Capitoline triad – Jupiter, between Juno and Minerva.

many others who appear merely to have been personified functions – but to us, and to Romans of the classical period, they are only names. They have *numen* (divine power) but no individual personalities. Though Roman religious observance was elaborate and detailed, and the calendar, all through the year, was full of sacrifices and rituals, administered by boards of priests, few have stories attached to them, and few of these, even when they purport to explain the particular cult or functional title of a god, involve the gods themselves. If there ever was a Roman mythology about their gods, it has vanished irretrievably. Roman gods lack personal adventures, and family relationships: for the great gods, these were simply taken over from the Greeks, Olympian and Roman deities being matched up in a very rough and ready way.

The principal Greek gods were **Kronos**, father of Zeus, who overthrew him; **Zeus**, king and weather god; his brother **Poseidon**, god of waters and earthquakes; **Hera**, queen goddess, wife (and sister) of Zeus, deity of marriage and women; and Zeus' other sisters **Demeter** (grain and crops) and **Hestia** (the household hearth). To these must be added the children of Hera, **Ares** (war), and **Hephaistos** (smith-craftsman), who was married to **Aphrodite**. She was the goddess of love, and variously said to be 'foam-born' from Kronos' father Uranos, or Zeus' daughter by a Titaness. **Athena**, goddess of wisdom, was daughter of Zeus and Metis (a personification of counsel). Other children of Zeus, by various lovers, were the twins **Apollo** (music – also medicine, archery, flocks and herds) and **Artemis**, associated with wild animals, hunting and virginity; and also **Hermes**, messenger of the gods, and patron of merchants and thieves, and a late-comer to Olympus, **Dionysos** (also called Bacchus), god of wine.

Some of these, though not all, the Romans simply identified with gods of their own, not always very appropriately. **Jupiter** (also known as 'Jove'), **Neptune**, **Mars**, **Venus** and **Vesta** are more or less good fits for Zeus, Poseidon, Ares, Aphrodite and Hestia. **Vulcan**, the Roman fire-god, is equated with Hephaistos. Artemis was identified with **Diana**, a goddess of woodlands, but also probably of the moon, women and child birth. **Juno**, though appearing historically in functions very like those of Hera, and especially as a goddess of women, may originally have been a deity associated with the vigour of young warriors. Kronos is ill-matched with the Roman **Saturnus**, originally perhaps a god of sown crops, who became associated, like Kronos, with a primitive Golden Age, before agriculture was necessary.

Minerva is also rather surprising as a match for Athena. **Minerva** was an Italian goddess of handicrafts. For the Romans, she was one of their chief triad of gods, Jupiter, Juno and Minerva, with a temple on the Capitol. The temple and its triad came to symbolise being Roman, and were reduplicated all over the Roman empire. The Romans themselves believed that it had been instituted, *c.* 509 BC, by Rome's last king, Tarquin the Proud. His father had come from Etruria, which may tell us something about Minerva's origins, while her elevation to a senior position, like Athena, perhaps reflects the influence of Greek culture on the Etruscans already at that period.

Mercury, the analogue of Hermes, was probably not originally Roman at all, but merely a renaming of a Greek god taken over by the Romans, along with a group of others, in the first decade of the fifth century BC. About the same time, Demeter and Dionysus were introduced to Rome as **Ceres** and **Liber**. This was done on the advice of the so-called *Sibylline Books*, a collection of oracles kept in the temple of Jupiter Capitolinus and consulted in times of crisis (particularly natural disaster, such as plague or famine) to discover how to make peace with the gods; the response was usually the introduction of a new god, or a new religious rite. Dionysius tells (following, he says, Varro) how the Romans came to possess them:

> A certain woman who was not a native of the country came to the tyrant [Tarquin the Proud] wanting to sell him nine books full of Sibylline oracles. When Tarquin refused to buy them at the price asked, she went away and burned three of them; then soon after she came back and asked the same price for the remaining six. She was thought mad, and was laughed at for asking the same price for the smaller number of books as she had failed to get even for the larger number, and she went away again and burned half the remaining books. Then she came back and asked the same price for the three that were left. Surprised at her determination, Tarquin sent for the augurs and asked them what to do. Certain signs told them that he had rejected a blessing sent by the gods. They declared that it was a great misfortune that he had not bought all the books, and told him to give the old woman as much money as she wanted, and take the remaining oracles.

He did, and the woman disappeared. Tarquin appointed keepers of the oracles, a post, says Dionysius, which existed to his day. When the oracles were destroyed by fire in 83 BC, a fresh collection was made by transcribing oracles from various parts of the known world; some of these were found to be fakes.

Rome was generally receptive to new gods and goddesses. Among the first to be admitted to Rome were **Apollo** (for whom no Roman equivalent was found), as healing god, and the deified hero **Heracles** (whom the Romans called Hercules). One of the most famous introductions was the Great Mother Goddess, **Cybele**, or Mater Magna, brought, in the form of a black stone, to Rome in 204 BC during the war against Hannibal; her temple was inaugurated in 191 BC, and an annual festival of theatrical performances and games, the Megalesia, established. The cult came from the 'Greek' end of the Mediterranean, from Phrygia in Asia Minor. The festival, at least, was highly popular among the Romans, though no Romans were allowed to participate in her cult, which did not conform to their ideas of decorum. It involved noisy street processions of ecstatic priests who leapt and danced, accompanied by horns, drums and cymbals, and begged from the passers-by. Abandoned dancing, specially in public, was disapproved of anyway by the Romans, and matters were made worse in their eyes by the fact that the priests were eunuchs.

What the Romans really thought about their Hellenised gods is all the more difficult for us to perceive because in surviving writings the stories have become little more than literary motifs or devices. Ovid in *The Art of Love* simply took over from Homer the story of how Vulcan (Hephaistos) caught his wife Venus and Mars (Aphrodite and Ares) in bed together, trapped them with an invisible net and fetched the other gods to laugh at them. Ovid uses it to illustrate some tongue-in-cheek advice to suspicious lovers: if you suspect she's cheating, don't try to catch her out – you'll lose in the long run. He hastily adds, '*Of course*, this isn't about real married ladies.' This was cautious: Augustus had introduced a law with stern penalties for adultery. He exiled Ovid in AD 8, for reasons which are unknown, but the erotic amorality of much of his poetry cannot have helped.

However, Virgil found it convenient in the *Aeneid* to ignore Venus' infidelity. She persuades Vulcan to make weapons for Aeneas (her son by a mortal, Anchises) by the simple use of marital seduction:

He hesitated, but she put her snowy arms about him and clasped him in a warm and tender embrace. And he suddenly took flame – as usual – and the familiar heat entered his marrow and raced through his trembling bones, just as when thunder cracks apart the storm-clouds and the fiery flash darts out, sparkling. The goddess was aware of it, pleased with her cunning and conscious of her beauty. The old god answered, bound in the toils of undying love.

He consents, conjugal relations (it is hinted) follow, and he falls asleep.

The seduction scene is almost a parody of one in the *Iliad*, in which Hera diverts Zeus' attention from what is happening on the Trojan battlefield. Virgil uses it for the purpose of introducing a description of the arms, particularly of the shield. This also is an idea lifted from Homer's *Iliad*, in which Hephaistos makes a shield for Achilles. Virgil wants to use the decoration on the shield for a sort of picture-show of famous events in Roman history, culminating, in the middle, with a splendid set-piece in which the future Emperor Augustus, Virgil's patron, and (as his publicity kept reminding Romans) descendant of Venus and Aeneas, is shown defeating Antony and Cleopatra at the battle of Actium (31 BC), with Apollo helping him – another myth in the making – and holding a triumph in Rome over conquered peoples from all ends of the world.

This terracotta architectural ornament represents Augustus' triumph. Victory carries a trophy of weapons, and stands on a globe flanked by Capricorns, Augustus' lucky sign.

Aeneas and the destiny of Rome

Aeneas is best known to the later world through the epic poem of Virgil, in which the hero's travels and travails are explicitly presented as a nationalist myth about the origins and divine destiny of Rome. In Homer's *Iliad*, Aeneas the Trojan already had a great future ahead of him; the god Poseidon rescued him from the battlefield, prophesying that he and his descendants would be kings. After the fall of Troy, Greek traditions took him, with his father Anchises and son Ascanius and some Trojan companions, to the West, like many other Trojan War veterans from both sides – so providing foundation legends for many places in Sicily and South Italy, where Greeks had been settling from the eighth century BC onwards.

Early history of the Aeneas legend

Already in the late sixth century BC, the story of Aeneas' flight from Troy was known in Etruria; it is depicted on a number of Athenian black-figure vases found there. The motif also appears on votive statuettes found at the Etruscan town Veii and on Etruscan gems. He is first associated with Rome by Hellanicus, a Greek historian in the fifth century BC, who wrote that Aeneas founded Rome and called it Rhome (Greek for 'strength') after one of the Trojan women accompanying him. Some Greek writers, however, ascribe the foundation not to Aeneas but to other Trojans and Greeks; in one version, Rome was founded by a son of Odysseus and Circe. Later Aeneas reappears, as father or grandfather of the founder of Rome.

It is not really surprising to find Romans willing to accept that their founders were foreigners. These stories enabled the Romans to claim their own place in the tradition, regarded as in a sense 'historical', of the Greek heroic past. As descendants of Aeneas the Trojan, in particular, they could still remain separate from the Greeks; better still, Aeneas in Italy appears as a friend and collaborator of Greeks, not their enemy.

There was an alternative tradition, that Rome was founded, not by Aeneas or any Trojan or Greek founder, but by Romulus and Remus. Some early Roman historians said that they were Aeneas' sons, or grandsons. However, it came to be realised that Aeneas, or even his grandchildren, really would not do as founders of Rome. When a Greek scholar, Eratosthenes of Cyrene (275–194 BC), constructing his universal chronology, *Chronographia*, fixed a date of 1184 BC for the Fall of Troy, the length of the gap between Aeneas and

Aeneas carrying his father Anchises and the Palladium (an image of the goddess Athena); coin issued by Julius Caesar, 49 and 47 BC.

Romulus became obvious. Various dates, ranging from 814 to 728 BC, were proposed for the foundation of Rome; the one which eventually became accepted was 753 BC. In the early second century BC, the elder Cato filled the gap ingeniously with what became in its main outlines the standard version.

Aeneas, arriving in Latium, at a spot called 'Troia', founded a city called Lavinium on land given him by the local king, Latinus, and ruled there with his wife Lavinia, the daughter of Latinus, over their united people, now called Latins. After Aeneas' death in a war with a local prince, Turnus, and the Rutulians (who, in Virgil, fight Aeneas *before* his marriage), his son Ascanius founded Alba Longa, which he later handed over to his brother (or, in some versions, son) Silvius, who was the first of a line of kings who conveniently filled the gap until the birth of Romulus and Remus, and, some years later, the foundation of Rome.

Following the prophetic trail

Every good foundation legend has to have portents and prophecies. In Virgil's story, following correct procedure for a Greek city-founder, Aeneas sailed first to Delos to receive a prophecy from the god Apollo, who told him, in typically obscure fashion: 'O descendants of Dardanus [mythical founder of Troy], the land which bore your first ancestors shall welcome you in its fertile bosom on your return. Seek out your ancient mother.'

Ascanius remembered that Teucer, an ancestor of the kings of Troy, had come from Crete, and there Aeneas and his Trojans sailed. In Crete he had a vision of the Trojan Gods, carrying a message from Apollo, who found it necessary to make his meaning plainer. The 'ancient mother' was Italy, for Dardanus had originally come from there. Sailing through the Ionian sea, the Trojans landed on the islands called Strophades. They slaughtered some cattle and prepared a meal, but were immediately attacked by the Harpies, monstrous bird-women, who fouled the food. The Harpies were beaten off, but their leader uttered a prophecy: 'You will go to Italy and be permitted to enter harbour; but you will not be granted a city, and gird it with walls, until, for the wrong you have done us, dire hunger forces you to gnaw and devour your tables.'

In Epirus they found a fellow Trojan, Priam's son Helenus, now ruling as king over a city created in Troy's image. He gave Aeneas detailed instructions for the voyage, and prophesied:

'I shall give you a sign; keep it stored in your mind. When, anxious and troubled, you shall find by the waters of a secluded river lying on the bank under holm-oak trees a huge sow, which has just farrowed, with her thirty young, a white sow, with her white offspring about her udders, that will be the spot. There you will find rest from your labours. And do not worry about the eating of the tables; the fates will find a way, and Apollo will be at hand if invoked.'

The sow and her litter represented the Latins. Originally, the thirty piglets appear to have been identified as the thirty peoples which traditionally made up the original Latin League, finally conquered by the Romans in 338 BC; the interpretation of the thirty piglets as thirty years appears to have been the contribution of Fabius Pictor, possibly motivated by the fact that the loyalty of some of the Latin communities to Rome faltered during the war against Hannibal. Virgil gives the developed Roman version of the myth of the sow and her piglets, in which the spot where the white (*alba* in Latin) sow farrows is Alba Longa. There had also been a rival claimant to the position of mother-city of the Latins. The town of Lavinium claimed to have been founded by Aeneas himself, who had brought there the sacred objects, the Penates (domestic gods) of the Roman People, to which Rome's senior magistrates paid a ceremonial visit once a year. Around 300 BC, according to the Greek historian Timaeus, there was a bronze image of the sow and her litter in the market-place of Lavinium; how long it had been there is unknown, but there were still traces of it left in Varro's day. For the Romans, however, the sow showed Aeneas the way to *their* mother-city, Alba Longa – and also helped justify their claim to traditional hegemony over the rest of Latium.

Both prophecies, about the sow and the eating of the tables, were duly fulfilled. After a visit to the Sibyl at Cumae in south Italy, the Trojans sailed

The 'Laurentine Sow' and her litter, a marble group (2nd century AD) from Lavinium, commemorating its legendary foundation by Aeneas.

The moment of Aeneas' arrival at the future site of Rome (Virgil, Aeneid, *Book 8), as imagined in 1675 by Claude Lorrain, who illustrated many incidents from the* Aeneid.

north and into the mouth of the Tiber, and landed to picnic on the bank. They were so hungry that, having finished all the food that was available, they began to eat the thin cakes of bread that (inspired by Jupiter) they were using as platters. 'What, are we even eating our tables?' said Aeneas' son.

Any Roman would recognize that as an omen. Aeneas realised that the prophecy was fulfilled. He and his men made their way to the local king Latinus, who, having just received a prophecy from his father, the god Faunus, that his daughter was to marry a stranger, welcomed Aeneas as his destined son-in-law. However, this brought about the wars and troubles that had also been prophesied for Aeneas, because the Rutulian prince Turnus had already claimed Lavinia, and had the support of Latinus' queen. Juno also interfered, sending a Fury to stir the queen to arouse Turnus and also the Latins against Aeneas. War broke out.

Aeneas had a dream vision of father Tiber, who told him: 'This is your assured home, this is where your gods belong,' and repeated the omen of the sow and her piglets, adding that within thirty years Ascanius would found a city, Alba. Meanwhile, to get out of his present troubles, he must go and ask help from King Evander, a Greek from Arcadia now settled in Italy.

Aeneas manned two ships and, as they were about to leave, they saw the omen of the white sow. Aeneas sacrificed her and her litter to Juno, then the

Trojans rowed upstream to the Tiber until they came upon Evander, his son Pallas, and the leading Arcadians sacrificing to Hercules. He received Aeneas kindly, remembering, Virgil tells us, how Anchises had visited Arcadia once with Priam. And so – for Evander's home was on what the Romans knew as the Palatine hill – Aeneas had arrived at the site of Rome.

Rome before Aeneas

Evander was the son of a Greek nymph Themis, called by the Romans Carmenta, because, it was said, 'Thespiodis' is Greek for 'prophetic singer', and *carmina* is Latin for 'songs'. He and his companions emigrated from Greece about sixty years before the Trojan War. The town he founded was called Pallantium, after his mother-city in Arcadia, but the Romans corrupted it to Palatium. He was said to have founded the festival of the Lupercalia, as well as that of Hercules.

Although he lived on the site of the future Rome, Evander was not the founder of Rome, only of a settlement on Rome's citadel, the Palatine (which is ignored in the legend of Romulus' foundation). On the way to his city he showed Aeneas various points of interest, such as the Carmental gate and shrine, the rock of Tarpeia, the Capitol (still rough woodland then, but felt to be the home of a god), the Lupercal, the Janiculum and Saturnia (citadels founded respectively by Janus and Saturn) and the Argiletum – all places whose names would have resonance for a Roman.

The Argiletum, in historical Rome, was the booksellers' quarter (so perhaps Virgil is making a sly joke). The name means simply 'clay-field', but there had to be a legend, so it was 'where Argos died'. Tarpeia and her rock we shall meet again: she came to a bad end. The Lupercal, 'Wolf's Cave', Evander explains is called after the Arcadian god Lycaean Pan (there was a Mount Lykaios in Arcadia). Mention of Lycaean Pan gives the game away. King Evander himself is no more than a literary invention by writers trying to find links between Rome and Greek traditions. Evander was the name of a minor deity worshipped in association with Pan in Arcadia. According to Livy and Tacitus, he introduced writing to Italy (after all, someone had to, and he was an immigrant among the aboriginal Italians).

Carmenta is an equally shadowy figure. Although she had a priest of her own, a shrine near one of the gates of Rome (called after her), and a festival on two days in January, like most Roman deities she had no story. Because of her name, writers called her a prophet, and say that she foretold the future greatness of Rome, fitting her in either as Evander's mother or his wife. Ovid, however, also cheerfully invents a different story out of a bogus etymology, to suit her cult, which had to do with childbirth. Varro said there were *two* Carmentes, Postverta (Backward) and Prorsa (Forward), in reference to the position in which the baby presented itself. Here is Ovid's story:

Once upon a time married women used to ride in *carpenta*, carriages, which I think also got their names from Evander's mother. Later the honour was taken from them, and every woman determined, since their men were ungrateful, not to carry on the line for them by having more offspring. Recklessly, to avoid giving birth, they secretly thrust out the swelling burden from the womb. They say that the city fathers reproved their wives for having dared such cruel acts. All the same, they restored the right that had been taken away. They ordered that now two sets of rites in honour of the Tegean mother [Tegea is in Arcadia] be held for both boys and girls alike. It is not allowed to bring leather into the shrine, lest the sacred hearths be defiled by dead things. If you have any love of ancient rites, be present at the prayers; you will learn names you never knew before. Porrima is placated and Postverta – either your sisters, or the companions of your flight, Maenalian goddess [another Arcadian reference]. One is thought to have sung of what happened in the past [*porro*], the other of what will come hereafter [*postmodo*].

There is actually a little bit of 'history' in all this, though it is nothing to do with Carmenta. In 394 BC, it is said, the city matrons contributed their gold ornaments towards a thank-offering to Apollo at Delphi after the capture of Veii, and were given the privilege of using *carpenta* at all times, as a reward. During

A carpentum *drawn by mules; the coin commemorates the grant of this honour to Julia Augusta (the name given to Augustus' wife Livia after his death) in* AD 22.

the Hannibalic War an emergency sumptuary law (215 BC) forbade the use of such carriages except on religious occasions; this law was repealed twenty years later, though the women did nothing more drastic than demonstrate in the streets in support of the proposed repeal. Much later, Julius Caesar tried to ease Rome's traffic problems by banning the use of *carpenta* to everyone except the Vestal Virgins and the most important priests.

Aeneas and Carthage

In the first six books of the *Aeneid*, before finally reaching Italy, Aeneas travels around in the Mediterranean world – allowing Virgil both to give him weird and wonderful adventures like those in Homer's *Odyssey* and to incorporate various references to Greek myth – and is repeatedly moved on by oracles, prophecies and dream visions. Though it is made clear by Virgil at the outset

21

Venus, disguised as a huntress, meets Aeneas *near Carthage (Aeneid Book 1), drawn by Claude Lorrain (1678).*

that Aeneas *will* reach Italy, and start the chain of events leading to the foundation of Alba Longa and later of Rome itself, the tension is maintained by having him harassed and hampered by the goddess Juno, and not only during his sea travels. As we saw, even after he reaches Italy, and is betrothed to the daughter of King Latinus, local peoples are roused to warfare against him.

Juno's implacable hatred against the Trojans is given two motivations. One is resentment that Aeneas' mother, Venus, not she, was awarded the prize in a beauty contest of the goddesses by the Trojan prince Paris. Virgil adds another, drawn from Roman history: Juno's partiality to Carthage, with whom Rome fought three major wars (the 'Punic Wars') between 264 and 146 BC. Carthage, of course, was founded by the Phoenicians not at the supposed time of the Trojan War, but over four centuries later, like Rome itself. Virgil, however, has the first building of the city actually taking place at the time when Aeneas was shipwrecked on the Tunisian coast. His mother Venus, disguised as a young huntress, met him and told him about the new city and its queen.

Her name was Dido, and her husband Sychaeus had been killed by her brother Pygmalion, prince of Tyre. In a dream, her husband's spectre told her what had happened, urging her to escape, and also told her where to find a buried treasure to take with her. She assembled a group of people opposed to the tyrant, loaded the treasure on to some ships that were in harbour, and sailed to

Africa, where they were engaged, at the time of Aeneas' arrival, in founding their new city, Carthage.

To ensure her son's safety, Venus made Dido fall in love with him. Juno acquiesced, hoping that Aeneas would stay in Carthage and so not fulfil the destiny that would lead to the foundation of Rome. Destiny, however, must not be thwarted. Jupiter sent his messenger Mercury to remind Aeneas of his obligations to posterity and warn him that he must leave. There was a terrible scene between Aeneas and Dido, in which she heaped reproaches upon him. Nevertheless he left, and Dido, before killing herself, uttered a prophetic curse, both on Aeneas himself and on his descendants:

'Thenceforth, Phoenicians, harry with acts of hate his stock, and all the race that will be; render this service to my ashes. Let there be no love nor treaties between our peoples. May some avenger arise from our bones to pursue the Trojan settlers with fire and sword, now or later, whenever the strength presents itself. Let shores be opposed to shores, I pray, waves to waves, weapons to weapons. May they battle, they and their sons' sons.'

Did Virgil also intend, it has sometimes been asked, to remind his contemporaries of another foreign queen who had recently been at war with Rome, Cleopatra of Egypt, the mistress of Mark Antony? She is depicted only briefly and unsympathetically in the *Aeneid*, on the shield made by Vulcan, at the moment of flight from the battle of Actium, surrounded by the outlandish gods of her country. Actium was an easy victory.

Whatever Virgil may have intended, what most people know or remember from the *Aeneid* is not the message of the divinely-directed destiny of Rome, culminating in Augustus, but the tragic love of Dido. In Ovid's poetry Dido recurs frequently, typifying the deserted lover; in his *Heroides*, imaginary letters from famous heroines, number 7 is from Dido to Aeneas. Chaucer includes her in his *Legend of Good Women*, calling her 'Dido the Martyr', and taking, he says, Virgil and Ovid as his sources. He ends by quoting Ovid's poem:

'Right so,' quod she, 'as that the whyte swan
Against his death beginneth for to singe,
Right so to yow make I my compleyninge,
Nat that I trowe to getten yow again,
For weel I woot that it is all in vain,
Since that the goddess been contraire to me.
But since my name is lost through yow,' quod she,
'I may well lose a word on yow, or letter,
Albeit that I shall never be the better;
For thilke wind that blew your ship away,
The same wind hath blowe away your fey [faith].'

If anyone wants the rest of the letter, he adds: 'Rede Ovide, and in him he shall hit finde.'

Christopher Marlowe wrote a somewhat stilted play about her, Henry Purcell an opera, or rather operatic and balletic entertainment. Three of the five acts of the grand opera by Hector Berlioz, *Les Troyens*, which he called 'Virgil Shakespeareanised', are about Dido and Aeneas.

How much of it was Virgil's invention we cannot tell. Timaeus says that Dido, still grieving for her dead husband, killed herself to avoid being forced to marry a Libyan king. Naevius, who wrote in the third century BC a Latin epic on the first Punic War, included Aeneas, but it is impossible to tell from the fragments that remain whether he had him visit Carthage. Varro, in his lost *Antiquities*, had Dido's sister Anna, not Dido herself, commit suicide for love of Aeneas. Nonetheless, it was Virgil's powerful telling of Dido's tragic love story that conquered the world's heart.

The *Aeneid* and Augustus: the legend brought up to date

However, the patriotic myth is uppermost. At the start of the epic, with echoes of Homer's *Odyssey*, Virgil presents Aeneas as a man with a mission:

Arma virumque cano – arms and the man I sing. Made an exile by fate, he was first to come from Troy to Italy, to the coast by Lavinium. He suffered many hardships both by land and by sea, through the might of the gods above, because of the grudge borne by cruel Juno, and he underwent much suffering also in war, until he should found a city, and bring his gods into Latium. Thence arose the Latin race, the fathers of Alba and the lofty walls of Rome.

Three times in the *Aeneid* Virgil introduces a reminder of the future destined for Rome. In Book 1 Jupiter utters a prophecy to allay Venus' fears. Aeneas shall die three years after fighting a successful war in Latium and settling his warriors.

'But the boy Ascanius, to whom now the additional name Iulus is given – he was Ilus, while the royal power of Ilium [i.e. Troy] survived – shall complete thirty full years of circling months in power, and will transfer the seat of power from Lavinium and fortify Alba Longa. Then there shall be three hundred years of rule by the kin of Hector [a Trojan prince] until Ilia, a royal priestess, pregnant by Mars, shall bear twins. Then Romulus, happy to be covered by the tawny coat of the wolf, his nurse, shall take over the people, build walls of Mars, and call his people Roman, from his own name. To them I set no bounds in time or space. I have given them empire without limit ... An age shall come when the house of Assaracus [Aeneas' mythical great-grandfather] shall crush to subjection even Phthia and illustrious Mycenae, and conquer Argos, and hold mastery there [i.e. the Trojans' descendants shall conquer the Greeks]. There shall be born a Trojan Caesar, of noble origin, who shall bound his rule with Oceanus, his fame with the stars, Julius, a name handed down from great Iulus. Some day you will receive him in heaven, laden with the spoils of the East; he also will be invoked in prayers. Then shall the harsh ages lay aside wars and grow gentle. White-haired Faithfulness and Vesta, Remus and his brother Quirinus shall make the laws. The dread gates of war, with their tight iron bolts, shall be shut; evil Frenzy seated within on a pile of cruel weapons, bound with a hundred chains of bronze knotted behind him, shall rave with bloody mouth.'

Another reminder, already mentioned, is the description of the shield in Book 8. Before that, the essence of Jupiter's prophecy is repeated in Book 6. After leaving Dido, Aeneas went first to Sicily, and then at last landed in Italy, near Cumae, where there was an entrance to the underworld. Guided by the Sibyl of Cumae, he went down to visit his dead father, who showed him a pageant of Rome's future greatness. At the beginning are the kings of Alba Longa, founded by a son of Aeneas; towards the end, famous heroes of Rome's Republican past. In between are Rome's founder, Romulus, and its 'second founder' Augustus.

A cameo with the head of the deified Augustus.

Thanks to Romulus' initial foundation, Rome shall grow great and populous. Next to Romulus is Augustus Caesar.

'Here, here is the man whom you have often heard foretold, Augustus Caesar, son of the Deified, who shall reestablish the golden age in Latium, where once Saturn ruled; he shall extend the bounds of the empire even past the Garamantes and the Indians, in land that lies beyond the yearly path of the sun and the constellations, where sky-bearing Atlas turns on his shoulder the sphere studded with blazing stars; even now the Caspian realms and Maeotic land shudder at the prophecies of the gods foretelling his coming, and the sevenfold mouth of the Nile is distraught and panic-stricken. Even Hercules, though he transfixed the brazen hind, pacified the Erymanthian woods and made Lerna tremble at his bow, did not visit so much of the world, nor victorious Bacchus, driving with reins of vines his yoked panthers from the high crest of Nysa.'

Augustus is compared with two gods, both of them late-comers among the Olympians and both, as it happened, the offspring of Zeus by mortal women (Romulus also had a divine father). In addition Heracles, in Greek myth, was deified as a benefactor to mankind, for having rid the world of so many monsters. Similar comparisons were made by other contemporary poets, such as Horace. The implication is that Augustus – if not actually a god already – deserves to be one.

Poetic flattery, perhaps, but overlapping with official propaganda. Augustus is called 'son of the Deified'. Julius Caesar's family traditionally claimed descent from Venus and Iulus, son of Aeneas. Augustus, who was actually only Julius' great-nephew (on his mother's side), inherited Caesar's property after his assassination. He took his name – from being C. Octavius, he became C. Julius Caesar ('Augustus' was an honorific name given him later) – and called himself his son. After the appearance of a comet during commemorative games, Julius Caesar was declared deified, and his 'son' henceforth called himself 'son of the Deified'. As we shall see later, Romulus also, according to one story, was taken up into heaven. After the deification, images of Julius Caesar had a crown with rays like the sun. When Augustus himself died in AD 14, a senior senator took an oath that after the cremation he had seen the form of the emperor ascending into heaven. He was officially declared a god, and his images acquired the radiate crown.

Founding fathers: Romulus and the kings of Rome

Just as Virgil's is the most famous of the stories of Aeneas and his arrival in Italy, so the best known account of the foundation of Rome is the one told by Livy. By his time this had long been accepted, in its essentials, as the 'canonical' story, though Greek and Roman writers in the past had produced many others. Of these nothing survives except what was said about the names and lineage of the founders. The most ingenious is that the Palatine was originally called Valentia because of the physical strength (*valere* is Latin for 'to be hale and hearty') of its aboriginal inhabitants; then when Evander and Aeneas arrived, the name was simply translated into Greek as 'Rhome'.

In earlier versions the founder is Aeneas himself, and if not him, then Rhomus or Rhome (the feminine form), occasionally Romulus (without Remus), and Rhomus/Rhome/Romulus is said to be the son of Zeus, or the companion, wife, daughter or granddaughter of Aeneas, or son of Odysseus or of Latinus, or of 'Italus'. Romulus and Remus (or Romus) start off as sons or grandsons of Aeneas, and are first mentioned in literary sources in the fourth century BC; it is very likely that oral traditions existed much earlier.

Romulus, Remus and the foundation of Rome

Aeneas' son founded Alba Longa, and the hereditary dynasty of its kings, all bearing the additional name 'Silvius', after his son Silvius. The eleventh in the line was Proca. He had two sons, Numitor and Amulius. Amulius usurped the throne from his elder brother, murdering his sons. He then forced Numitor's daughter, Rhea Silvia, to become a Vestal Virgin, so that Numitor might have no male descendant. Rhea Silvia was raped, and bore twin boys. She said Mars was their father, either because she really thought so, or because it seemed more respectable if a god were responsible for her lapse. Cruel Amulius had her imprisoned in chains, and ordered the boys to be thrown into the river.

The job was sloppily done, the boys being left in slow-moving floodwater in a basket which went aground, under the Ruminal fig-tree (two different trees in ancient Rome were said to be *the* tree). A she-wolf found them and suckled them. Then a shepherd Faustulus took them home for his wife Larentia to nurse. Some say that she was actually a common prostitute (*lupa*, in Latin slang; it also means 'wolf'), and that that was how the wolf got into the story.

Plutarch knew a different story. The house of Tarchetius, king of the Albans, a most lawless and cruel man, was visited by a supernatural apparition. A phallus rose out of the hearth and remained for many days. He consulted an oracle of Tethys in Etruria, which gave the reply that a virgin must have intercourse with the apparition, for from her would be born a son who would be most renowned for his valour and surpassing in good fortune and in strength. Tarchetius told the prophecy to one of his daughters and ordered her to have intercourse with the apparition; but she thought it beneath her dignity, and sent a maidservant instead. Tarchetius was furious and arrested both the women, intending to put them to death, but the goddess of the hearth appeared to him in his sleep and forbade the murder. He kept them in prison and set them to weave a piece of cloth, telling them that when they finished they were to be given in marriage. So they spent the days weaving, but at night, on Tarchetius' orders, other women undid their work. When the maidservant, who was pregnant by the phallus, bore twins, Tarchetius gave them to a certain Teratius with orders to kill them, but he took them to the riverside and left them there. A she-wolf visited them and suckled them, and all sorts of birds came and put food into their mouths. At last a cowherd found them and took them to his home, and when they grew up, they overthrew the wicked king.

When they grew up (in Livy's version), Numitor's grandsons formed a gang and took to robbing robbers, and sharing their spoils among the shepherds. The robbers took exception to this, captured Remus in an ambush during the festival of the Lupercalia, and told Amulius that he and Romulus were to blame for the cattle raiding that had occurred on Numitor's land. Remus was handed over to Numitor to be punished.

Matters were desperate. Faustulus revealed the circumstances of his finding the babies; Numitor began to put two and two together, and the young men were acknowledged. With the other herdsmen they raided the palace and killed Amulius, while Numitor seized the citadel, and was reinstated as king.

Alba was becoming overcrowded, so the brothers decided to found a new city, near the spot where they had been left to drown. With the same sibling rivalry that had caused trouble in their grandfather's generation, they quarrelled over who should be the official founder, and give his name to the city. They asked the local gods to declare by augury (that is, to give a sign by the observed flight of birds). Romulus took up position on the Palatine hill, Remus on the Aventine. Remus had a sign first, six vultures; then twice the number appeared to Romulus. Their respective followers claimed each of them as king, Remus because he saw them first, Romulus because he saw more birds. A fight broke out, in which Remus was killed.

Another story is told however, a more common one. Remus made fun of his brother and jumped over the partly-built walls. Romulus lost his temper and killed him, saying, 'So perish anyone else who shall jump over my walls.'

OPPOSITE The personification of Rome; a furniture ornament of silver, with gilding (4th century AD).

Mars descends to Rhea Silvia, accompanied by cupids; handle of a silver patera.

The history of the tradition

Clearly, there were two traditions about the founding of Rome, one the 'Greek' tradition involving Aeneas, the other a 'Latin' one, of Romulus and Remus (with an 'Etruscan' variant). Eventually, the two were combined, and in due course inventions, significantly lacking in detail, were added to fill the gap that chronological likelihood was discovered to require. Archaeology belies the story that Rome was a colony founded in the fifteenth generation from Alba Longa; earliest remains at both sites are from the same period. The 'Greek' tradition, as we have seen, goes back at least to the fifth century BC. The 'canonical' version combining the two and with expanded chronology appeared towards the end of the third century in Fabius Pictor, and before him in a Greek writer, Diocles of Peparethus.

However, there is still debate about when the homegrown version with the twins arose, and why. Was it a traditional tale, or a late, literary invention?

That is harder to answer than it looks, for many of the elements in the story that look like traditional mythical components are known to us best through Greek myths, and so could be, in the Roman story, the products of Greek literary invention – the rape of a virgin by a god; the attempt by a king to forestall a threat to his rule, involving danger to the child; the rescue and rearing in humble circumstances; even, perhaps, the twins, and the fratricide.

This does not mean that the kernel of the story, the identity of the founder, is not genuinely local and ancient. The connection with Aeneas is found in the archaeology of Etruria and in the writings of the Greeks, and he is also linked with Lavinium. The 'Roman' tradition, however, links itself with Alba Longa which in historical times was still, in an indirect way, a kind of 'religious capital' for the whole of Latium. One of the annual duties of Roman consuls was to hold the Latin festival on the Alban Mount, part of its former territory. Rome regarded itself as a Latin city; the takeover by kings from Etruria was a transitory, and regrettable, episode in its early history, and in due course Rome conquered Etruria.

Romulus, then, was a 'Latin' founder, from Alba Longa. When and why did he acquire a twin? One founder is enough. Various modern explanations have been offered: the twins are said to have originated in Indo-European creation myth; or the dual consulship in Rome; or two separate communities thought to have existed in early times on the Palatine and the Quirinal; they have even been compared with Cain and Abel. A recent suggestion is that Remus came into the story quite late, and because of Roman politics.

The invention of the twins

The earliest surviving representation of the wolf suckling the twins is carved on the back of a bronze mirror made in the late fourth century BC. In 296 BC the city of Rome itself acquired a public monument. The plebeian brothers Gnaeus and Quintus Ogulnius, magistrates in that year, secured the conviction of several

31

Faustulus, the wolf, the twins and the figtree: coin of 140 BC (the moneyer's name was Sex. Pompeius Fostlus).

moneylenders, and used the treasury's share of their confiscated property to embellish Jupiter's shrine on the Capitol and improve the approach to Mars' temple. They also set up, beside the famous fig-tree near the Palatine, the Ficus Ruminalis, a statue-group of the infants being suckled by the wolf. About a quarter of a century later, that image began to appear on Roman coins.

Now, between 367 and 296 BC Roman government had undergone a conversion, in which the Ogulnii had played a part, resulting in power-sharing between the two groups making up the Roman citizen body, the patricians (the old nobility) and the plebeians. Remus, whose name in Latin is associated with slowness, came into the story, it is suggested, during this period, to symbolise the late entry of the Roman plebeians into political power. But why kill him?

Archaeology may help. In 295 BC the Romans won a victory at Sentinum against two of their fiercest opponents, the Samnites and the Gauls. The plebeian consul Publius Decius Mus secured victory by deliberately dedicating himself to the gods, and being killed by the enemy. On the Palatine was a temple of Victory, dedicated a year after the battle. Under the foundations of the temple was a recent grave – possibly a human sacrifice. The death of Remus can be seen as combining, in legend, both these sacrifices for the safety of the city. Just one year later a temple was dedicated to Romulus, deified as Quirinus (a title also attached to Janus, Mars, Jupiter and Hercules).

Remus dies and the survivor becomes a god; in that way both are taken out of politics. Perhaps myth-making was at work, cementing reconciliation between patricians and plebeians.

All this, of course, is modern speculation about how the Roman founding myth developed, but there might just be something in it. 'Quirites' was what the Romans called themselves in their civilian role, so Romulus – Quirinus could be thought of as protector of the whole Roman people at peace. The elder Pliny (first century AD) wrote that outside the temple of Quirinus there were once two myrtle trees, one plebeian and one patrician. The patrician tree flourished while the Senate dominated Roman government, but then it withered and the plebeian tree flourished, 'about the time of the Marsic War', that is, 91–90 BC. The sixty years after that war, until the battle of Actium, saw a long series of political conflicts, erupting more than once into civil war.

The sites of the legend

Whatever its ancestry, Romans of the classical period 'knew' that the true story was the one about the twins and the wolf; they had the landmarks to prove it. There was the Wolf's Cave (Lupercal) on the side of the Palatine. The Greek story was that it was the shrine of Arcadian Pan Lycaeus ('Wolfish' Pan); for the Romans, it was named after their famous wolf, and that was where the priest sacrificed at the festival of the Lupercalia.

Near it was the fig-tree, the Ficus Ruminalis. *Ruma* or *rumis* was said to be an old Latin word for a breast, and there was a goddess of nursing mothers, Rumina, so, naturally, the fig-tree with its milky juice had sheltered the wolf foster-mother and the twins. Only vestiges of the tree on the Palatine survived when Ovid wrote. Inconveniently, there was another Ficus Ruminalis near the Roman Forum (which in AD 59 withered and then resprouted), but that was easily explained. It grew alongside a large boulder (probably a meteorite), which was regarded as sacred, and its correct name was 'Navius' Fig-tree'. Rome's fifth king, Tarquin the First, after a victory against the Sabines, decided to change Romulus' original organisation of the cavalry by adding extra units bearing his own name. A famous augur, Attius Navius, objected that this must not be done without first ascertaining divine will by taking the auguries. Tarquin was annoyed and jeered, 'Come on then, seer, divine whether what I am thinking of now can be done.' Attius took the auspices and declared that it certainly could.

'Ah,' said Tarquin, 'but what I had in mind was that you would cut through a whetstone with a razor. Take these, and do what your birds foretell can be done.' Without more ado, Attius did it. A statue of Attius was set up on the spot, beside the steps of the Senate-house, and the whetstone was put there

Some idea of the appearance of the 'hut of Romulus' can be got from this terracotta funerary urn (8th–7th century BC) from Monte Albano in the shape of a rustic hut.

33

too. Tarquin dropped the idea of the reorganisation (though he did increase the cavalry in numbers), and ever afterwards the Romans never did anything of importance to the state without first taking the auguries, and abandoned their intentions if the birds refused consent. As for the fig-tree, some said that it *was* the Ficus Ruminalis, which Attius by his special skills had transplanted to the Forum.

In Augustus' day there still stood on the Palatine hill a 'hut of Romulus' said to be the very hut of Faustulus, in which Romulus spent his youth, and the spot from which he took his augury. It was made of sticks and reeds, with reed thatch, and its remarkable survival over the centuries was because the Romans constantly made good the ravages of time and weather with new materials.

Romulus gets brides for the Romans

Romulus had founded a city, making the perimeter large to allow for expansion. Next he had to find enough population. He opened a sanctuary offering asylum and attracted a large number of refugees from neighbouring peoples. However, that solved the problem only for one generation; there was posterity to think of. He sent envoys around to all the neighbouring cities asking for alliances and intermarriage between their peoples, but they all refused, telling the envoys to set up a refugee sanctuary for women too if they wanted them. Something had to be done, because Rome's young men were growing restless and angry, so Romulus made a plan.

He arranged a festival in honour of the god Consus and invited the neighbours. They came flocking in their curiosity to see the new town, and the Sabines, in particular, turned out en masse, with their womenfolk and children. They were entertained in local houses and given a tour of the town, and then the show started. When the visitors' attention was absorbed, the signal was given, and the young Romans grabbed the young women and carried them off. Mostly it was first come, first served, but the aristocrats, naturally, had previously booked the prettiest girls, and their subordinates went and fetched them.

One of the best-looking was snatched for an aristocrat called Thalassius, and since people kept asking for whom she was being taken, her captors shouted, to keep people off, 'For Thalassius', and that is why the Romans shout 'Talassio' at weddings. Or, Plutarch the Greek remarks, it may have been from the Greek word for spinning (that is, if the Romans used the word), because

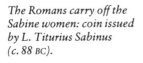

The Romans carry off the Sabine women: coin issued by L. Titurius Sabinus (c. 88 BC).

The intervention of the Sabine women, painted in 1799 by Jacques Louis David.

once the Romans and the Sabines were friends again, it was agreed that their wives should do no work for their husbands except spinning. (Later on it was a joke, as if that was all a wife was for.) And brides are still carried over the threshold because the Sabine women *had* to be; they did not go of their own accord.

The Romans, however, behaved like gentlemen. Romulus reassured the young women that they would be properly married, and honourably treated. What really won them over, though, was when the young men insisted that they had acted out of passionate love. The parents, however, were not happy. The Sabines, under their king Titus Tatius, laid siege to Rome, and the treachery of a Roman girl, Tarpeia, allowed them to capture the citadel. Romans and Sabines began to slog it out in the marshy ground between the Capitol and the Palatine hill.

Then the Sabine women rushed between the two armies, appealing to them. 'If you resent being related by marriage, turn your anger against us. We are to blame, we are the cause of injury and death to our fathers and husbands, and we would rather not live, than be widows and orphans.'

It worked. The two sides were reconciled, and Tatius and his Sabines were incorporated into Rome. If this story seems familiar, it is because the plot was used for the musical *Seven Brides for Seven Brothers*.

Livy's version emphasises the politics, the establishing of a stable community, and plays down the sexual violence. Ovid's approach is typically frivolous. In *The Art of Love*, Book I ('How to make it with Girls'), he recommends the gathering at the games as a good hunting-ground. It has been a hallowed custom, he says, ever since Romulus started it with the Rape of the Sabines.

The end of Romulus

Romulus ruled for nearly forty years, though he was more popular with the common people and the solders than with the Senate (or so said those later annalists who took the 'popular' side in politics). One day Romulus was reviewing his troops in the Campus Martius (near where the Pantheon is now). There was a sudden storm, with thunderclaps, a thick cloud hid him from everyone's sight, and no one ever saw him again. Some of the Senators standing nearby said that he had been swept away by the tempest, though there were some who secretly said that he had been torn to pieces by the Senators. The soldiers hailed him as father of his country, and as a god, Quirinus. One man did what was needed to secure belief in the deification and to calm people's panic and hostility to the Senate. A farmer from Alba, Julius Proculus (so the Julian family gets into the story again), who was in Rome for the day spoke to the people.

'Quirites,' he said, 'at first light this morning Romulus, father of this city, suddenly came down from the sky and presented himself before me. I was awestruck and stood there reverently. "Go," said he, "and tell the Romans that it is the wish of those in heaven that my Rome shall lead the world; tell them to perfect their military skill, and know and teach their children that there is no human power that can withstand the might of Rome." Then he departed aloft.' And so Romulus was declared to be a god.

Quirinus had an ancient shrine on the Quirinal hill, and a *flamen*, a special priest, but no temple until the end of the fourth century BC. Romans of the classical period thought (because the Sabines had a town called Cures) that Quirinus was a Sabine god, that the Quirinal hill took its name from an ancient Sabine settlement there and that 'Quirites' as an epithet for the Roman people came from the Sabine element incorporated into the citizen body.

The kings of Rome

Rome's next king was a Sabine, appointed by the people on the Senate's recommendation. His name was Numa Pompilius, and he was famous for his piety and knowledge of religious ritual. Later Romans thought of him as a philosopher king and some Greeks said (against chronological probability, even if he had been a real person) that he had studied under Pythagoras. He diverted the Romans from thoughts of war to the institutions of peace by establishing priesthoods, the religious calendar, and the proper ritual of religious observance. These he learned, or so he said, from a goddess, Egeria, his wife and adviser, who used to meet him at night and instruct him in religious lore. In order to *elicit* from the gods what portents from visible signs such as lightning were to be acted upon, and how, he dedicated an altar on the Aventine to Jupiter Elicius and consulted him by augury.

Numa found out from Jupiter the correct sacrifice to expiate a lightning strike. Getting a god to yield up his knowledge was not an easy matter, but Numa was his match in cunning. Ovid tells us that the tops of the trees on the Aventine quivered, and the earth subsided under the weight of Jupiter. The king's heart fluttered, the blood receded all over his body and his hair stood on end. When he recovered himself, he said, 'King and father of the gods on high, tell the sure method of expiating thunderbolts, if with pure hands we have touched your offerings, and if it is a pious tongue that asks now for this.' The god granted his prayer, but spoke with alarming ambiguity.

'Cut off a head,' said he. The king said, 'We shall obey. We must cut an onion, dug up in my garden.'

Then Jupiter added, 'A man's.' 'You will have,' said Numa, 'his hair.' Then Jupiter demanded a life, and Numa said, 'Of a fish.'

So, Numa, as befitted a king of peace, had outwitted Jupiter who, apparently, expected human sacrifice. However, the god was not offended. He laughed and said, 'You, man who are not to be scared off from talking with the gods, see to it that you expiate my thunderbolts with these things. But to you, when tomorrow's sun god shall have brought forth his full orb, I shall give sure pledges of empire.' Then he vanished in a thunderclap.

The Romans did not entirely believe Numa when he told them this, but they assembled the next day, and when the sun was fully up, Numa prayed to Jupiter and asked for fulfilment of his promise. Thunder came from a clear sky and a strangely shaped shield, indented in a curve on either side, fell from the sky.

Since this shield was the fortune of Rome, for security's sake Numa had eleven others made exactly like it, to deceive a thief. Only one craftsman, Veturius Mamurius, proved equal to the task. Numa also appointed a priesthood, the Salii, or Leaping Priests, to look after the shields. They were priests of Mars, and every year at the beginning of March, before the campaigning season, they paraded through Rome, performing a curious dance, and chanting a song of such antiquity that no one in Rome understood it any more, though

A coin showing two of the sacred shields; between them is a flamen's hat.

the priests continued to perform it year after year. We have the words, more or less garbled, as they were carved on marble recording the celebration of the ritual in Rome in AD 218, and there is still no certainty about the meaning, except that Mars is invoked.

Rome's next king, the warrior Tullus Hostilius, who incorporated Alba into Rome, was less fortunate in his dealings with Jupiter. The divine displeasure with his constant warfare was shown by a hail of stones, followed by a plague, and when Tullus secretly tried to use Numa's expiation ritual, he got the procedure wrong, and he and the palace were consumed by lightning.

The next king, Ancus Marcius, whose maternal grandfather was Numa, combined the interests of his two predecessors, and, it is said, introduced the concept of the 'just war'. In a ritual which was still practised in a modified fashion in the second century AD, war was formally declared on another country only after a Roman priest had visited its territory, calling each person he met, and Jupiter himself, to witness that satisfaction was demanded in the name of religion and justice. He was said to have brought water to Rome by aqueduct (his supposed descendant, Q. Marcius Rex, built the Aqua Marcia in 144 BC and was honoured with an equestrian statue).

Rome's last three kings, Tarquinius the First (an Etruscan immigrant), Servius Tullius and Tarquinius the Proud are in a more recognisable historical context, though this does not mean that all that writers say about them is true. Servius Tullius, in particular, appears partly as a political reformer, but also as a mythical figure. The circumstances of his infancy were legendary, and those of his death the stuff of melodrama.

As a little boy, Servius lived in the elder Tarquin's palace. One day, while he was asleep, flames were seen to play about his head, without harming him. When he awoke, they went out. Tanaquil, the queen, recognised this as a sign from heaven and told Tarquin that it meant he would be a support to their house. They accordingly reared him as a prince, and Tarquin betrothed him to his daughter. The story would be even better if he had been the child of a slave, but Livy, as always sceptical, cannot bring himself to believe that – a slave's child would never have been betrothed to a princess. His mother was obviously of high rank, a prisoner of war, who was befriended by the queen.

However, Ancus Marcius' sons, whom Tarquin had tricked out of the throne, resented his preferment and tried to assassinate Tarquin. While he lay dying, Tanaquil arranged matters so that Servius took over the reins of government, and in due course became king. Despite all the good he did for Rome, his end was unhappy.

Tarquin the First had two sons, Lucius Tarquinius, who was ambitious, and Arruns, who was not. They were married to Servius' two daughters, both called Tullia, and similarly different in character. By the good fortune of Rome, the two fierce ones were not initially married to each other. However, the bad Tullia turned the wicked Tarquin against her wimpish husband and his meek wife. Two murders later, she and Tarquin married, and then she began to egg him on against Servius. Tarquin bought support among the nobles with promises of favours, then threw Servius out of the Senate-house. As he staggered along the street, he was assassinated.

As Tullia's carriage was driving back towards her home on the Esquiline after she had been to hail her husband as king in the Forum, the driver pulled up short at the sight of Servius' mutilated body. Seizing the reins herself, she drove over her father's corpse, spattering her clothes and the carriage-wheels with blood. And that is how the street where it happened (the modern Via di S. Pietro in Vincoli) got the name Sceleratus Vicus, 'Street of Crime'.

Her husband Tarquin the Proud behaved as tyrants traditionally always behaved. He denied Servius burial and executed his supporters in the Senate. He exercised a reign of terror, inflicting death, exile or confiscation of property on those he disliked or whose property he coveted. Then a neighbouring town, Gabii, was taken over by Rome; historical writers simply plagiarised a story from the Greek Herodotus to flesh out the event. Tarquinius' son Sextus seized control of the town by trickery, and sent to ask his father what he should do next. The messenger reported that the king said nothing, but merely walked up and down in the garden, knocking off the tallest poppy-heads with his stick. Sextus understood.

The end of the monarchy

Tyrants usually violate the community's standards of sexual morality in some way. It was Tarquin's son, Sextus, who provided the last straw that made the nobles' resentment of Tarquin flare up into open rebellion and brought the monarchy to an end. He raped a noble Roman lady, Lucretia, who killed herself after telling her father and husband. Tarquin and his family were driven out of Rome and the people elected their first two consuls; the traditional date of this event was 509 BC.

That was not quite the last of the Tarquins. The deposed king obtained help from some Etruscan towns, and in particular from the king of Clusium, Lars Porsenna. Porsenna's siege of Rome produced a number of striking examples of Roman heroism and patriotism, and in the end, or so the Romans liked to believe, Porsenna was so impressed by these virtues, and by the Romans' stubborn resistance and determination to preserve their liberty, that he voluntarily withdrew.

The alternative history: Etruscans at Rome

This was a good story, but it was a cover-up. Tacitus and the elder Pliny knew that Porsenna had captured Rome and held on to it for a time. Besides, the archaeological evidence indicates that the Etruscans did not withdraw from Rome until the middle of the fifth century BC. Far from trying to restore the Tarquins, the king of Clusium apparently had had his own expansionist plans, and his eventual expulsion from Rome was achieved by the combined forces of the Latins, with help from the ruler of Cumae. However, this story was less flattering to Rome, and many preferred to ignore it in favour of a version that stressed the admirable qualities of the Roman national character.

There are traces, too, of other legends that indicate that Etruscan influence on early Rome was more thorough and long-lasting than most Romans were willing to admit. An exception was the emperor Claudius (AD 41–54), a keen antiquarian, whose first wife was of Etruscan descent, and who wrote a book on Etruscan history. In a typically long-winded and rambling speech to the Senate in AD 48, he justified the proposal to admit citizens from Gaul to office by recalling how Rome had admitted outsiders in the days of the kings. According to him, the Etruscans said that the king between the two Tarquins was not Servius, but a certain Etruscan, Caelius Vibenna, previously known as Mastarna.

A wall-painting in an Etruscan tomb at Vulci, from the fourth or third century BC, illustrating a story whose details are lost to us, shows Mastarna freeing Caelius Vibenna, while Aulus Vibenna fights someone from Falerii and another man kills Gnaeius Tarquinius Rumach ('from Rome'?). 'Mastarna' seems to be only the Etruscan word for 'magistrate'. But Aulus Vibenna at least is a real Etruscan name – it is found on a pot of the sixth century BC from Veii. Caelius Vibenna was known to Varro as an Etruscan noble (he gave his name, of course, to Rome's Caelian hill) who helped Romulus against King Tatius and the Sabines, and Varro said that the Tuscan Way in Rome was named after his followers. According to some Romans, including Cicero, the name of one of the three Roman tribes created by Romulus, the Luceres, came from another Etruscan king who helped Romulus against Tatius.

These scattered references to an 'Etruscan' history of Rome may have some basis in Etruscan cultural, if not also political, expansion into Latium at an early date. However, the Sons of the Wolf preferred to stress their Latinity, and to give credit for their success to themselves and to the gods.

The hero and the state

Every Roman schoolboy was taught the legends of early history, which exemplified the virtues that the Romans liked to think were part of the essential Roman character, and stressed in particular the principle that the welfare of Rome must come before the desires of the individual, and even before loyalty to the family group. The noblest Roman families were particularly proud to include such stories in their family histories, and, at least during the Republic, continued for a long time to model their conduct upon them. Stories of this sort were a staple component of the orations delivered at public funerals, to inspire the young men to emulation. Ennius, the author in the third century BC of Rome's first national epic, the *Annales*, wrote: '*Moribus antiquis res stat Romana virisque*' ('Upon the values and the men of old Rome stands firm').

Ennius' appeal was to traditional values, his context historical. In 340 BC the consul Titus Manlius Torquatus (said to have acquired the last name as a young man, when he fought a Battle of the Champions against a huge Gaul, slew him, and took the torque from his neck) was in command of a Roman army against the Latins. His son, stung by the taunts of a Latin cavalry commander, against orders engaged him in a duel. Torquatus, upholding military discipline, had his son executed immediately. In 140 BC his descendant found that his son, whom he had given in adoption to another Roman, had abused his position as governor in Macedonia to extort money. He publicly refused ever to see him again, and when his stricken son hanged himself the next night, he refused to attend his funeral but spent the day, as usual, in the atrium of his house seeing those who came to seek his expert advice on civil law and pontifical ritual. The story is in a collection of such moral anecdotes, 'Memorable Deeds and Sayings', published in the generation after Augustus by Valerius Maximus, who says that Manlius, like other noble Romans, kept wax images of his ancestors, including the stern Titus, as a reminder to live up to their standards.

The Torquatus of 340 BC had a legendary precedent. When Tarquin the Proud was expelled from Rome, certain young Romans, including the sons of Lucius Junius Brutus, one of Rome's first pair of consuls, formed a plot for his restoration. The plot was discovered, and they were all sentenced to death. The father did not spare his own sons; indeed, as consul, he was present, seated on the official dais, during their execution. No one paid attention to the others; all eyes, said Livy, were upon him, and upon his sons.

This model of stern subordination of personal and family interests to those of the state is not specific to one form of government. Among the Romans it is

*Bronze figure of a lictor
(magistrate's attendant).
The bundle of rods and axe
he carries symbolise the
magistrates' power to inflict
punishment, including the
death penalty.*

found in stories attached both to the period of the kings and to the early Republic. It is interesting that a later period also found it adaptable. One of the most famous paintings of the French Neo-classical artist Jacques-Louis David shows the consul Brutus sitting in his house, eyes downcast, while the lictors carry in the bodies of his sons. It was exhibited at the Paris Salon in 1789, several weeks after the storming of the Bastille, but it had been commissioned by the monarch.

Horatius and the Battle of the Champions

Even more famous is David's *The Oath of the Horatii*, which shows three brothers apparently resolving to fight to the death. Although later interpreted, in view of David's active participation in post-revolutionary politics, as a rallying call to the masses, it was in fact painted for the Crown some five years before the revolution as part of a project, supervised by Louis XVI's minister for the arts, for improving public morality through the use of the visual arts. The oath-scene was David's invention; it is not in the ancient story, nor in the play about the Horatii by the seventeenth-century French dramatist Pierre Corneille. The power of David's concept has made it a cult image. *Le Serment des Horaces* has been adopted as the title of a French journal launched in 1987 specialising in university research on art history.

David's picture emphasises readiness to sacrifice one's own life for the state. The ancient story includes other elements, and in particular one which would not have fitted well into the French king's didactic scheme – he would scarcely have wished to seem to sponsor sororicide.

The Romans under Tullus Hostilius, their third king, fought a war against the Albans which ended in the demolition of their city and their incorporation with the Romans. The kings of Rome and Alba agreed that, to conserve their manpower against their common enemy, the Etruscans, they should settle the issue by a Battle of the Champions. Conveniently, in each army there were triplets, the Roman Horatii and the Alban Curiatii, and they agreed to fight.

On the appointed day, for the first time known to tradition, the solemn agreement between the Romans and Albans was made by the 'fetial' procedure. The priest, bearing an uprooted plant, asked and received the king's consent to act for Rome. Then he touched with the plant Spurius Fusius, who was to utter for the Romans the formula of the oath not to depart from the terms of the treaty. 'Should they do so with evil intent and by public consent then, Jupiter, may you strike them even as I strike this pig, and the more so, in that your power and might surpass mine.' So saying, he killed the pig with a flint knife. The Albans likewise took the oath.

The champions stepped forward, watched anxiously by both the assembled armies. All three of the Albans were wounded; but then first one, then a second Horatius was killed. The last Horatius turned and ran – not, however, through cowardice, but to separate his opponents. He killed the first pursuer, then the second as he came up. The third, exhausted, could offer no

The Oath of the Horatii, *painted in 1784 by Jacques Louis David.*

resistance and was killed with a single stroke. Both sides buried their dead; their graves, said Livy, were still to be seen. Horatius received the weapons and cloaks of the Curiatii as his spoils, and marched back to Rome at the head of the Roman army.

He was met by his sister, who had been betrothed to one of the Curiatii. When she recognised the cloak she had made for him, she loosened her hair in mourning and shrieked his name. At once, Horatius stabbed her to the heart. 'Take your childish love to your betrothed. You have no thought for your brothers, living and dead, and for your country. So perish all Roman women who mourn for an enemy.'

The people were in two minds. Horatius' deed was dreadful, but at the same time, he was a national hero. He was put on trial before the king, who used the archaic procedure for *perduellio* (literally 'treason' – since Horatius had pre-empted the people's right to pass judgement), which Livy explains for his readers. If Horatius was found guilty even after appeal to the people from the magistrates' decision (*provocatio* – an ancient right of the citizen), he was to be blindfolded, hanged on a barren tree, and his corpse scourged.

The appeal went to the people. Horatius' father spoke. Had his daughter not deserved her death he would have exercised his right as a father to punish his son himself, but he begged the people that his heroism in the fight should save him. Horatius was acquitted, but his father had to perform certain rites of expiation for him, and Horatius had to pass with covered head beneath a beam slung across the road.

There was a spot in the Forum known in Livy's day as 'the Horatian Spears'; that was where, it was said, the spoils of the Curiatii had hung. Close to where the Colosseum later stood, there was a beam (*tigillum*), replaced from time to time at state expense until at least the fourth century AD, known as the *Tigillum Sororium*. This is explained as 'the Sister's Beam' from *soror*. Near it, however, were two altars, to Janus Curiatius and Juno Sororia, and the Roman religious calendar mentions a ceremony at the spot on 1 October. This suggests that false etymologies may have produced a legend to explain primitive and obsolete rituals accompanying rites of passage for the young boys of the *curiae* (ancient voting-groups of the people) and the girls reaching puberty (*sororiare* meaning the growth of breasts), as well as to account for one or two traditional topographical names. The legend also, as told in classical writers, inculcated certain values – country before life, patriotism before personal affection.

How one-eyed Horatius kept the bridge

Lars Porsenna and the Etruscan army marched upon Rome, heading for the vulnerable point, the wooden bridge across the Tiber. The Roman guards began to flee in panic but another Horatius, called Cocles ('One-Eyed'), urged a few of them to break down the end of the bridge while he did his best to hold off the enemy single-handed. Two noble Romans, Spurius Larcius and Titus Herminius (both, interestingly, names of Etruscan derivation) stayed out of shame, and helped Horatius by prolonging the resistance for a few precious minutes; he sent them back when the bridge was almost cut through, then turned to try to continue holding off the enemy until the work could be finished. His taunts actually nonplussed them for a few moments, then a shower of spears came. Horatius caught them all on his shield. As the whole army advanced, the bridge suddenly crashed down, cutting off his escape.

Calling upon father Tiber to save him, he jumped in full armour into the river and swam across. He had saved Rome, and his reward was a statue (the first, says the elder Pliny, ever set up in honour of an individual) and a plot of land. Some private individuals, Livy adds, voluntarily contributed to his maintenance during the hard times of the siege that followed.

Horatius was not always saved by his swimming. In another version, Horatius deliberately sacrificed himself for his country – and there is no mention of public honours. Indeed, there is something suspicious about the story of a public statue for a living person at so early a date. Horatius' leap into the river from the Pons Sublicius, Rome's oldest bridge, is reminiscent of a mysterious ceremony on 14 May when the Roman pontiffs, the Vestal Virgins and the praetors threw thirty straw puppets, called Argei, into the river from this bridge. Again, we may have an example of a legend growing up to explain a ritual, and perhaps also an old cult-statue, and being given also a moral dimension.

One of the most popular poems in English literature, for generations after its publication in 1842, was Lord Macaulay's 'Lay of Ancient Rome' about Horatius. Macaulay's Etruscans show a tinge of British sportsmanship; when Horatius struggled out onto the bank, 'even the ranks of Tuscany / Could scarce forbear to cheer.'

How Scaevola lost his hand

Another traditional type of tale, found also among the Greeks, is that of the secret mission behind the enemy lines. Porsenna's siege of Rome continued and food was running short. The humiliation of Rome's suffering siege, especially by an enemy who had so often been defeated in the past, determined a young aristocrat, Gaius Mucius, to undertake a great risk; but first he sought permission from the Senate (otherwise the Roman guards might take him for a deserter and kill him). Armed only with a dagger, he made his way by stealth into the Etruscan camp. The king was sitting on a platform with his secretary, and pay was being distributed to the soldiers.

Which was the king? They were dressed so much alike that Mucius could not be sure. Taking a chance, he stabbed the wrong man, and was promptly seized and hauled before Porsenna. He hurled defiant words at the king, threatening obscurely that the king need never think himself safe. When Porsenna ordered him to tell what he knew, on pain of being burned alive, Mucius cried, 'Look! See how little men think of their bodies, when their eyes are set on great glory,' and he thrust his right hand into a lighted altar-fire and held it there, as though insensible of the pain. Porsenna was so impressed that he ordered him to be set free, as a gallant enemy. Mucius, in a rather curious form of thanks, volunteered the information that three hundred young nobles had sworn to undertake this mission in succession, until one of them should succeed. The immediate result of his exploit was that Porsenna opened negotiations with the Romans, which led to peace. Mucius thereafter bore the *cognomen*, additional name, Scaevola, 'Left-handed', which in historical times belonged to a particular branch of the clan of the Mucii.

This story can be no earlier than the third century BC, and bears obvious signs of Greek influence. Romans in the sixth century BC did not generally bear a *cognomen*, despite the genealogical fancies of later generations; besides, *scaeva* (an omen from the left) was known to Romans of Varro's day as a Greek loan-word, and the adjective *scaevus* does not enter literary Latin until the second century AD. Porsenna's well-dressed secretary is another Greek touch, and the secret mission may owe something to an Athenian legend of their early king Codrus (who went to the enemy camp to be killed, in order to fulfil an oracle and save his country).

The story helps to motivate the withdrawal of Porsenna from Rome, which, as we saw, was the preferred Roman version of the history of their

Scaevola burning his hand before Lars Porsenna: Italian majolica plate, c. 1510–20.

relations with the Etruscans. It was fabricated for the family traditions of the patrician Mucii Scaevolae, a family which in the later Republic shows historical and antiquarian interests. The first one known to history was praetor in 215 BC. In the second century BC two Scaevolae, father and son, were in succession Pontifex Maximus, chief priest at Rome, and so had access to a primitive form of chronicle, the *Annales Maximi*, the chief priest's annual records of festivals and other events. A century later another member of the family helped to organise Augustus' antiquarian revival of the Saecular Games (traditionally commemorating at intervals of about 110 years the foundation of Rome.)

Naturally, the Scaevolae would want to devise an acceptable explanation for their family name, either because left-handedness was regarded as unlucky in ordinary life (though lucky from the point of view of Roman augurs), or because, as the story perhaps suggests, it laid itself open to the obvious insinuation that an ancestor had had his hand burned off as a punishment.

Ironically, the Romans came to use the story of Scaevola as part of the pageantry of punishment. By the first century AD executions by various means, and other forms of corporal punishment, were not only included as part of the entertainment in arena displays, such as wild-beast shows, but even incorporated into theatrical performances. Such performances occurred at the grand inauguration in AD 80 of the emperor Titus' new amphitheatre, the Colosseum. The poet Martial describes one charade where someone apparently was allowed the option of burning his hand off as an alternative to being burned to death inside a tunic covered in pitch:

> The other day at the morning show
> We saw Mucius put his hand in the fire.
> If you think that he was enduring and tough,
> You must be as thick as a man from Abdera.
> If they say, with the itchy shirt there, 'Burn your hand,'
> It takes a great deal more guts to say 'No'.

So a legend meant to illustrate patriotic self-sacrifice was adapted as a sensational way of demonstrating the authority of the state.

The story of the belly and the limbs

Less than twenty years after the expulsion of the king, Rome faced a double crisis, external threat from the neighbouring hill-peoples, and internal strife between the common people and the ruling class. The people revolted in protest against the cruel law which allowed creditors not only to seize the property of their debtors, but to imprison and maltreat them. Promises to change the law were not kept. There were riots, and only with the greatest difficulty was the Senate able to enrol the army to face the threat of invasion. When, however, fearing sedition at home once the army was disbanded, the Senate tried to keep them mobilised and on campaign, the whole people marched out of the city and camped three miles away on the Sacred Mount. This was known as the first Secession of the Plebs.

The Senate sent a plebeian, Menenius Agrippa, to reason with them, and he told them a parable, the story of the Belly and the Limbs.

'In the days when all the parts of a man did not, as now, agree together, but each limb had a mind of its own and could speak for itself, the other parts complained that it was unfair that they had to worry and exert themselves to provide everything for the belly, while the belly stayed quietly in the middle, doing nothing but enjoy the pleasures with which it was provided. So they conspired together that the hands should not convey food to the mouth, nor should the mouth accept what it was given, nor should the teeth chew up what they received. They intended, in their resentment, to subdue the belly in this way by starvation; but what happened was that every one of the members themselves and the body as a whole almost completely wasted away. And so it had become apparent that the belly too was not idle but performed a service, that it was no more nourished than it nourished them, returning to all the parts of the body what we depend on for life and health, when it is allocated equally among the veins, and made ready by the digestion of food – that is, the blood.'

The people recognised the parallel between the intestinal dissension in the body and their own resentment against the Senators. A compromise was agreed, and they were given magistrates of their own to protect them against arbitrary action by the consuls. And so the first tribunes of the plebs were appointed, one of them Sicinius, leader of the revolt.

Coriolanus and the siege of Rome

However, the harmony between the people and the Senate did not last long. Agriculture had been neglected during the secession, and the city was on the verge of famine. Corn had to be imported from far and wide for the next two years. The price would have to be subsidised if the people were to afford it, and there were some Senators who wanted to make the people give up their newly-won political privileges in return.

One of the most vehement spokesmen for this point of view was Gaius Marcius. He was a national hero. The previous year, as a junior officer, he led an attack on the Volscian town of Corioli and captured it, earning the name Coriolanus. Now, however, he antagonised the people against both himself and the Senate. 'I would not put up with King Tarquin,' he said, 'am I to put up with King Sicinius? Let him secede and call the plebs away to the Sacred Mount and the other hills. No one is stopping them. The prices are their own fault; let them put up with them. I dare say they will soon knuckle under and till the fields themselves, rather than secede under arms and prevent cultivation.'

The tribunes promptly summoned him for trial. The Senate were terrified. At first they tried to use their personal bully-boys to prevent the people from having meetings; eventually, they resorted to begging them to let Coriolanus off. He, however, failed to appear in court and the people sentenced him to exile (so Livy writes; Plutarch, on the other hand, has a dramatic trial scene in which Coriolanus' contemptuous behaviour further antagonises the people).

Coriolanus went to his old enemies, the Volscians, who were for the moment at peace with Rome. He conspired with one of their leaders, who by using disinformation and black propaganda panicked the Senate into ordering the immediate departure of the Volscians who were in Rome to attend a festival. Then they saw to it that this diplomatic incident blew up again into open war by the Volscians against the Romans.

Coriolanus personally led the Volscian army. First he recaptured the Volscian territories recently taken by the Romans, and then overran Latium, finally laying siege to Rome itself. Twice the Senate sent envoys to negotiate with him; the second time he refused even to give them a hearing. They sent their priests, with no more effect. Then the women of Rome appealed to Coriolanus' aged mother Veturia and his wife, Volumnia. When Coriolanus heard that they had come, with his children, he went to embrace them. His mother held him off: 'Are you my enemy or my son? Am I your mother, or a prisoner of war? When you saw Rome, did you not think of your home with its gods, and of your family? If I had had no son, Rome would not be in danger. My

Coriolanus reproached by his mother: Italian majolica dish, 1544.

misery will not last long; but think of the others who will die or become slaves.'

Then his wife and children clung to him sobbing, and the women with them broke into tears. Coriolanus was completely overwhelmed. He sent them home and withdrew the army; but whether the Volscians killed him or he spent a long life in unhappy exile, no one knew for certain.

That is the story as told, rather baldly, by Livy, under the evident influence of a source reflecting the 'popular' politics of a section of the Senate in the first century BC, but without overt criticism of either side. Livy goes no further than to suggest that Coriolanus' intransigence was not in the best interests of the Senate: with more willingness to compromise they might have got rid of the tribunate.

The best stories, however, are adaptable to suit the interests and purposes of a variety of tellers. For Plutarch, the motivating force of Coriolanus, whose father had died in his boyhood, was a desire to please his mother (called Volumnia in this version), and he showed towards her all the filial respect which he would have shown a father. His Coriolanus is paired with the Athenian Alcibiades (who also turned traitor in exile), and given some qualities to enhance the 'match'. Coriolanus, like a tragic hero, is in large part to blame for his own downfall, because of his pride and unrestrained aggression and intolerance, and he goes into exile bent on avenging himself on Rome. Plutarch's version is much more dramatic and emotional in the telling, and it is not surprising that it is the one which inspired later writers.

Shakespeare in his *Coriolanus*, both to conform to the political orthodoxy of his own day and to bolster Coriolanus' credibility as a tragic hero, gives his contemptuous arrogance some justification by developing a hint in Plutarch and presenting the people's leaders as mean-spirited, manipulative trouble-makers. On the other hand, for the Communist Bertolt Brecht, who left an unfinished play, *Coriolan*, at his death, Coriolanus is far from a hero. His mistaken pride in believing himself indispensable and irreplaceable is exposed; the common people of Rome, united, can well do without him.

Family fictions, and how history repeats itself

Every great Roman family had its own collection of family legends. Here are two from the early and middle Republic.

The Fabii were a distinguished family in the early Republic. Every year from 485 to 479 BC one of the consuls was a Fabius. During most of those years Rome had waged an indecisive war against Veii, an Etruscan city, and Rome's rival for control of vital trade routes along the Tiber valley. The Veientes frequently raided the Romans' fields, escaping before the legions could draw them into pitched battle. Other wars threatened, and the legions were needed elsewhere. Then the Fabian clan went to the Senate and said, 'Leave the Veientes to us. We will wage this war as if it were a family feud, at our own expense.'

The whole city turned out to see them march forth, 306 in number, with their leader, one of the consuls of the year (478 BC). They set up a garrison in a fort on the frontier, on the river Cremera, and there they stayed, fighting frequent skirmishes against the Veientes. But the latter devised a plan. They would sometimes leave flocks and farmhouses unguarded; their armed men, if they encountered the Fabii, would run away as if in panic. At last, the Fabii grew contemptuous of their enemy and over-confident; and so one day, as they chased some unguarded livestock, they were caught in an ambush. The date was 13 February. They were all killed – all, that is, except one, scarcely out of boyhood, in whom the Fabian line was kept alive.

That was the family story. There were some debunkers among the Greek writers, who said the Fabii were not alone, but part of a legion with four thousand others; Dionysius calls it a story 'like a fiction of legend or the theatre'. The numbers involved, and the year, are suspiciously close to those of the Spartans holding off the forces of Xerxes at the Battle of Thermopylae.

Lustre was added to the family history of the Decii by the action for which several generations were renowned. In 340 BC, before a battle against the Latins (the same battle in which the son of the consul Titus Manlius Torquatus engaged the enemy against orders, see p. 41), the sacrifice offered by the other consul, Publius Decius Mus, boded ill for his family. When the wing under his command began to be driven back by the enemy, Decius instructed a pontiff to dictate to him the formula for *devotio* (self-dedication) to the gods, so that he might save his legions.

He put on a purple-bordered toga, covered his head and, standing on a spear and touching his chin with one hand, he recited the formula. He called upon Janus, Jupiter, Mars, Quirinus, Bellona, Lares, gods new and gods native, gods of the Romans and of their enemies, and gods of the underworld, that they might prosper the might and victory of the Roman people, the Quirites, and afflict their enemies with terror and death. 'As I have uttered the words, even so on behalf of the Republic of the Roman people, the Quirites, and of the army, the legions and auxiliaries of the Roman people, the Quirites, I do devote myself – and with me the legions and auxiliaries of the enemy – to the gods of the underworld and to earth.'

He then adjusted his toga in the ritual 'Gabine manner' and rode into the midst of the enemy. The enemy were thrown into confusion and the Romans given fresh heart; and as Decius fell beneath a hail of missiles, the tide of battle turned.

Fifty-five years later, at the battle of Sentinum against a combined force of Gauls and Samnites, Decius' son, in his fourth consulship, devoted himself in exactly the same way. That was the decisive battle of the third Samnite War, and effectively settled Rome's leadership of Italy.

So far, so good; but Cicero knew of a story that the grandson followed the example of his father and grandfather at the battle of the Aufidus in 279 BC. Other sources, however, mention this Decius as still alive in 265 BC. Perhaps his *devotio* did not 'take' and he survived, in which case, according to Livy, the proper ritual was to bury a life-size effigy in the ground instead. The drawback was that the unsuccessful self-devoter could never again take part in any religious ritual.

Alternatively, the commander need not devote himself at all; he could 'volunteer' any citizen from the legions. Perhaps the third Decius simply felt that the family tradition was getting out of hand.

Legendary ladies

There were also legends about Roman women, both good and bad. We may find these more attractive than those about the self-denying heroes, but although they sometimes contain romantic or even tragic elements, a closer look will show that, for the Romans, they had the same original purpose as the stories about Rome's male heroes, that is, to encourage acceptance of Roman moral priorities, in particular self-control and self-discipline, in the interests of the Roman state and its security.

Tarpeia the traitress

Let us begin with a wicked lady, Tarpeia. A story was needed to account for the traditional name of a rock near the south-western end of the Capitoline hill in Rome.

The bare story can be told in two sentences. When king Tatius and his Sabines were laying siege to Rome in order to recover their kidnapped women-folk, Tarpeia, daughter of the Roman commander, who had gone outside the walls to fetch water, agreed to let the Sabines into the Capitoline citadel. Once inside, they threw their shields upon her and killed her.

Here the complications start. Why did Tarpeia let the Sabines in? In the straightforward Tarpeia-the-traitress version, the motive was greed. Tarpeia had agreed to betray the citadel for gold. She coveted the heavy golden armlets and rings worn by the Sabines, but when she claimed as reward 'what you wear upon your arms' (meaning the jewellery), she was instead crushed under the Sabines' heavy shields.

Propertius, a poet contemporary with Virgil and Ovid, gave the story a romantic-seeming twist (which owed a good deal to a Greek myth well-known to Roman poets) by making Tarpeia fall in love with the king as she saw him riding out in full armour. Her price for betrayal was to become Tatius' bride; the outcome, however, when she tried to claim payment, was the same, her death. To Romans, however, love was no more acceptable as a motive than lust for wealth, especially when it conflicted with patriotic duty. Propertius makes it clear that Tarpeia deserved what she got – even the Sabine enemy condemned her crime – and he heightens her guilt by following the version of the story that made her a Vestal Virgin, vowed to chastity.

There was another version of the story, in which Tarpeia was not a traitress but a heroine, acting from the highest motives. This Tarpeia planned

A coin showing Tarpeia already waist-deep in a pile of Sabine shields.

the destruction of the Sabines. When she asked for 'what they bore upon their left arms', her intention was to deprive them of the defence of their shields, and to raise the alarm for the Romans; but the Sabines saw through the ruse, and killed her. We may think her incredibly naive, but that is beside the point. Tarpeia the heroine was said to be buried at the spot bearing her name. At any rate, annual libations were made there, and this story accounted for them.

On the other hand, the Tarpeian rock had a sinister reputation. Those convicted of particularly serious offences were executed by being thrown down from it. Which offences, other than treachery, our sources do not specify, and historical instances are hard to find. In AD 33, a man from Spain was so executed on a charge of incest with his daughter, but, Tacitus says, the emperor, Tiberius, really wanted to get hold of his gold and bronze mines. In any case, this evil association required an appropriate story to account for it – hence Tarpeia the traitress, with her individualistic and unpatriotic desires.

A nice girl

Much more healthy and wholesome was the story of Cloelia (from a family which claimed several consuls in the first century of the Republic). When Lars Porsenna agreed to withdraw from Rome after Scaevola's exploit, he demanded a number of Roman hostages, who were kept in the Etruscan camp near the Tiber. Among them was an unmarried girl called Cloelia. She organised a group of fellow hostages, all girls, and led them in swimming across the river – 'among the missiles of the enemy' says Livy – and so restored them to their families.

Once again, Porsenna was torn between anger and admiration, and this time the etiquette of warfare complicated matters. Porsenna declared that her exploit outdid the likes of Horatius Cocles and Scaevola. If, as a hostage, she was not returned, he said, he would regard the treaty as broken; but, if she was returned, he undertook to send her back intact and inviolate to her people. The Romans returned her, and then Porsenna was better than his word. He presented her with half the hostages, at her choice. She chose, it is said, the boys who had not yet reached puberty, for two reasons. One was that that was more seemly in a young girl (that is, than to choose sexually mature males); the other, that boys of that age were particularly vulnerable to abuse. When peace was made again, the Romans rewarded this valour, unusual in a woman, with an equestrian statue on the Sacred Way.

The horse arrives in the story rather awkwardly, though the story is used to account for the statue, which was a Roman landmark. The original statue was replaced after being destroyed by fire in 30 BC. Horse-riding is no more probable than swimming as a normal activity for high-class and, it seems, sheltered, young Roman ladies in the early Republic. The story, as told by Livy, combines several functions. It is part of the proud tradition of a noble family; it explains a statue; and, like the story of Scaevola, it helps to explain why Porsenna left Rome. Besides all these, it carried some clear messages about the moral attitudes and sexual behaviour to be regarded as desirable – as well as some sinister hints about the treatment which both young women and young boys lacking the protection of free status or parental presence might expect to receive in Rome.

Behaviour and reputation

Great store was set upon the chastity of Roman women, and in none was it more important than in the Vestal Virgins, guardians of the sacred hearth of Vesta, whose purity was at once the symbol and the guarantee of the welfare of Rome. Death by entombment alive in an underground chamber was the punishment inflicted several times during the Republic on Virgins found (usually in times of national crisis) to have been unchaste.

Suspicion was easily provoked. In 420 BC, it was said, Postumia, whose brother had recently been fined for his part in a Roman defeat at Veii, was charged before the priests with sexual immorality. She was innocent, as it happened, but had acquired a doubtful reputation because she was rather too well-dressed and smartly got-up, and showed unsuitable independence of mind. She was judged innocent and let off with a warning. In future, the chief priest told her, she should stop making jokes, and pay more attention to holiness than to fashion in her choice of dress.

Some lucky ones had their chastity miraculously vindicated by the gods. Aemilia, a senior Virgin, had left the fire in the care of a new member, who had allowed it to go out. When the fire was found to be out, there was a great to-do in the city, and the priests decided to investigate whether Aemilia had been unchaste. She stretched out her hands toward the altar and prayed to Vesta: 'If for nearly thirty years I have devoutly and properly carried out all my sacred duties, keeping a pure mind and a chaste body, manifest yourself to help me, and do not allow me to suffer a wretched death; but if I have done any impious deed, let me cleanse the city by my punishment.' She tore off a part of her robe and threw it on the fire. From the cold ashes, a great flame sprang up.

Or there was Tuccia, who, under a similar charge, said that she would prove her innocence in deeds. She walked down to the river Tiber; the whole of Rome turned out to watch. Then, after asking Vesta's aid, she took up water in a sieve and carried it all the way to the goddess's shrine, without spilling a

*Head of the Vestal
Aemilia, on a coin issued
by an Aemilius in 65 BC.*

*A marble head of a Vestal Virgin,
showing the special arrangement of
her hair, a style otherwise worn only
by brides on their wedding-day.*

drop – or, some say, to the Forum, where she poured it on the ground at the feet of the priests – whereupon her accuser mysteriously disappeared and was never seen again.

Claudia and the Great Mother

One of the highlights of the Roman year was the week-long celebration, in early April, of the Megalesia ('Great Games'), the festival of Mater Magna ('Great Mother'), or Cybele. The story of the introduction of the goddess to Rome involved members of the most prominent families, one of them a woman. In 204 BC, during the war against Hannibal in Italy, plague was rife in the army, and there were more ill omens than usual. The Sibylline books were consulted, and the usual remedy proposed – the introduction of a new cult. A prophecy was found which said that a foreign invader in Italy could be driven out if Cybele was brought from Pessinus in Phrygia to Rome. Five Roman senators went as envoys to King Attalus in Pergamum and received the sacred black stone which represented the goddess. A special boat was prepared, and the stone made the long journey across the Mediterranean until it reached the mouth of the Tiber. Ovid's version of what happened next is the most dramatic.

All the knights and the stately senators, mingled with the common people, came to the mouth of the Tuscan river to meet her. With them came in procession also mothers and daughters and brides and the Vestal Virgins. Men wearied their arms tugging at the tow-rope, but the foreign ship could scarcely make headway against the stream. There had been a long drought; the ship's keel grounded on the muddy shallows. Everyone strained to the utmost, chanting to help the effort, but the ship stuck fast, like an island in mid-sea. It was a portent; stricken, they stood shaking.

Claudia Quinta traced her descent all the way from the original Clausus, and she had beauty to match her noble ancestry. She was chaste, but that was not her reputation. Unfair rumour had injured her, making false charges. What told against her was her dress and make-up, and the elaborate hairdos with which she appeared – that, plus her readiness to answer back to severe old men. She knew she was innocent, and laughed at the lies told about her – but people in general are ready to think the worst.

She stepped forward from the line of chaste matrons and took up pure water from the river in her hands. Three times she poured it on her head, three times she raised her hands in the air – everyone watching thought she had gone out of her mind. She knelt down, her hair loosened, and gazing at the goddess's image she said:

'Fruitful mother of the gods, graciously accept a suppliant's prayer, on this condition. They say I am not chaste. If you condemn me, I will acknowledge guilt, and pay for it with my life. But if I am free of blame, demonstrate my innocence. You are chaste; follow my chaste hands.'

She gave a slight tug on the rope. This is a strange tale, but stage-plays also testify to what I say. The goddess moved; she followed her leader, and in so doing approved her.

The story had been presented in plays (probably at the festivals) and was presumably popular. There was, however, another, rather duller story. The oracle had said that the goddess was to be welcomed by the best of the Roman men and the best of the women. The senate chose as best of the men a young man who had not yet actually started on a magisterial career but who (probably not coincidentally) was cousin of the Scipio who was consul in 205 BC and went on to command the victorious final campaign against Hannibal in Africa. 'What exactly were the virtues on which they based their judgement,' says Livy rather drily, 'I would willingly pass on to posterity, if only chroniclers of that time had been specific; however, I do not intend to hazard any guesses of my own about something that was so long ago.'

Claudia (whose other name, 'Quinta', suggests that she was the youngest of five sisters) belonged to the same great Roman clan as one of the two censors of 204, the men responsible for letting the contracts for the building of the new goddess's temple. Whether the censor's influence had something to do with a relative being chosen as 'best of the women' we can only guess. Her nomination would make another honourable entry in the family's history.

The 'popular' version was perhaps originally started by someone hostile to the family, but it made a much better tale. It was also much more useful for moralising purposes, since it went into specifics. Decent women did not question the opinions of the senior men of the community; and decent women did not doll themselves up. Why should they wish to appear attractive to men other than their husbands? This was the conventional view presented by many Roman writers (though Ovid, in his intentionally 'shocking' erotic poems often takes the opposite stance). Men disciplined themselves; women had to be coerced into being good. How in the past Roman men had instilled proper ideas of behaviour was shown by several (probably apocryphal) stories – e.g. of a woman allegedly starved to death by her family for having taken the keys to the wine-cellar, or one divorced for going to the games without her husband's knowledge, or another for appearing in public unveiled.

When the story of the dashing Claudia first appeared is not known. In the first century BC Cicero ignored it, but that does not mean that it did not exist; the other version suited his purpose better. His political enemy, Publius Clodius, a descendant of the great family, had a sister, a 'merry widow', who was thought to be the real instigator of a charge of poisoning against Cicero's friend, Caelius, in 56 BC. In his defence speech, after imagining the ghost of another famous ancestor, Appius Claudius the Blind (censor 312 BC), upbraiding Clodia for her behaviour, Cicero puts his own interpretation on her life-style. 'Let us suppose,' he says, 'a woman – not *her*, of course – who gives herself to anyone and parades her lovers; who allows all sorts of self-indulgence in her private park, her Roman mansion, her beach house at Baiae; who gives money to young men' – who, in short, is a brazen hussy and spendthrift, with the habits of a whore. What had Clodia done to lay herself open to this? Appearances were against her, as against Claudia Quinta. She was rich, and entertained a lot; she had a house at a holiday resort, and went about publicly with young men. She was a widow, but she had neither taken herself out of circulation nor – the next best thing – remarried.

Divorce in Rome was frequent and easily obtained by both sexes, and remarriage by widows and divorcées generally expected. Nevertheless, the persistent moral ideal, however little honoured in practice, was the *univira*, the 'one-man woman', that is, the one who went straight from girlhood's virginity into marriage, and had relations with no other man for the rest of her life. In a society where all the women were *univirae* the men would no doubt have been able to feel more secure. Two more stories – one of them still famous today – show indirectly something of the underlying anxieties of Roman men.

Tyranny, lust and revolution: Appius and Verginia

The Claudii were one of Rome's oldest and noblest families, and they were proud of their history. In 79 BC, a Claudius who was consul had shields inscribed with his family's achievements set up on the walls of the temple of Bellona, the War-Goddess, founded almost three hundred years before by his ancestor, Appius Claudius the Blind.

However, there was at Rome an equally powerful anti-Claudian tradition that accused them of ingrained arrogance and overweening behaviour towards the people. One of the worst, so the story went, was Appius Claudius the Decemvir, consul in 451 BC. He was one of the committee of ten men (*decemviri*) set up in that year to produce Rome's first codified law. The result was the Twelve Tables; ten were produced in the first year, and two more in 450 by another committee of ten; only Appius was a member of both. This second committee, at the instigation of Appius, refused to resign after its work was done, or to hold elections, and began a reign of terror in Rome.

Appius lusted after a plebeian girl – some accounts call her, aptly, Verginia, and her father Verginius – who was already betrothed to a plebeian political activist, Icilius. When Appius failed to seduce her, he instructed one of his dependants, Marcus Claudius, to claim her as his slave. The man accordingly seized her one morning, as she entered the Forum with her attendant, calling people to witness that she was his slave. He brought her into court; Appius, of course, was trying the case.

Verginius was away with the army and unable to make a defence, and the case might have gone by default, but pressure from the bystanders forced Appius to agree to defer judgement till the following day. However, since her father was not there to take custody of her, Appius and Marcus should retain her overnight. Verginia's fiancé strongly resisted this – he knew what treatment a female slave might expect – and called on the Romans to support him. 'I am to marry her, and I intend to have a virgin as my bride. You have enslaved the people by depriving them of their political rights, but that does not mean that you can behave like owners and exercise your lust on our wives and children.'

Appius backed down for the time being and allowed Verginia to remain free overnight. Her friends hastily summoned back her father. Appius' letter ordering the army commanders to detain him arrived too late, and Verginius was there in court the following day. Appius, however, did not even allow him to make his counter-claim, but immediately pronounced in favour of Verginia's alleged owner, quelling any possibility of riot among the crowd by drawing attention to the presence of his armed escort. He granted Verginius' request to be allowed to question his daughter's attendant, in Verginia's presence.

Drawing them to the side of the Forum, Verginius grabbed a knife from a butcher's shop and stabbed his daughter to death, crying, 'Only so can I make you free!' Verginius escaped to the army and incited them to revolt, while Icilius and Verginia's uncle incited the urban populace. The result was revolution. The *decemviri* were overthrown and the people were once again able to elect their tribunes, to protect them against arbitrary coercion by magistrates.

The rape of Lucretia

Tyranny, lust and revolution are also the ingredients of one of the best-known stories from antiquity; this is Livy's account. In 509 BC King Tarquin the Proud started a war against Ardea. The cause was his own extravagance. His ambitious building schemes had drained the public funds, and he needed booty also to appease the people's resentment of the servile labour he had made them perform. During the siege of Ardea, as the king's sons sat drinking one night with their kinsman Collatinus, they argued about which had the best wife. At Collatinus' suggestion, they decided to ride back to Rome to catch their wives unprepared and find out what they were doing in their absence.

The princes' wives were found enjoying lavish dinner-parties with friends.

The suicide of Lucretia, an engraving by Marcantonio Raimondi, after a design by Raphael, c. 1511–2. The Greek inscription means: 'It is better to die than shamefully to live.'

Then the husbands rode to Collatia. There Lucretia was found busy in the activities which were typical, Romans liked to believe, of old-fashioned virtue. She was at home, seated among her slave-women, still working, late though it was, at her wool. Collatinus had won; but Lucretia's proven chastity, as well as her beauty, had quickened the lust of Sextus Tarquinius, son of the king.

A few days later, Sextus made a secret visit to Collatia and was received as a guest. That night he went with drawn sword to Lucretia's bedroom and awoke her. He declared he loved her, pleaded, threatened, but to no avail. Then he said that he would kill her and a slave, and leave the slave's naked body beside her, to make it look as if she had been caught and killed in the act of adultery. Lucretia gave in. After the rape she sent messages summoning her father and her husband to come, each with a friend; Collatinus brought Lucius Junius Brutus. When Collatinus asked, 'Is it well with you?' she answered, 'What can be well with a woman who has lost her chastity? The mark of another man is in your bed. But only my body has been violated. My mind is guiltless, as my death shall testify. Swear that you will take vengeance on the adulterer.'

All the men swore, then began to try to comfort her. She was forced, they said, so it was not her fault. It is the mind that sins, not the body, and where there was no intention, there is no guilt. Lucretia answered: 'You may decide what *he* deserves. I absolve myself of wrongdoing, but I do not free myself from punishment; and hereafter no unchaste woman shall live through my example.'

Then she stabbed herself through the heart with a knife which she had hidden in her dress. Her kinsfolk collapsed in grief, but Brutus seized the dripping knife and swore to destroy the Tarquins and abolish the monarchy. Brutus had survived under the rule of Tarquin the Proud (and so, it is said, obtained his 'brutish' *cognomen*) by pretending to be stupid and harmless; now he threw off the pretence. With Collatinus and Lucretius he took Lucretia's body to the Forum and there made a speech inflaming the people against the Tarquins. The result was revolution, and the beginning of the Roman Republic.

Lucretia: the later life of a legend

The story has exercised a fascination on artists and writers for two thousand years, from Ovid, who, though otherwise close to Livy, emphasises the erotic aspect by elaborating on Lucretia's feelings at the moment of the rape, to the present Poet Laureate, Ted Hughes. It is the subject of one of Shakespeare's two long poems (the other is *Venus and Adonis*), which Hughes sees as religious myths, acting as templates for the construction of all Shakespeare's plays from *All's Well That Ends Well* to *The Tempest*.

Many writers, such as the English dramatists Thomas Heywood and Nathaniel Lee, the Protestant reformer Heinrich Bullinger in sixteenth-century Switzerland, and Voltaire in France, wrote plays giving greater prominence to Brutus and the overthrow of the monarchy than to the fate of Lucretia. In Shakespeare, the political dimension is barely present; he concentrates on the confused internal debates of Tarquin and, especially, Lucretia, complicated by the addition of Christian ideas of sin and guilt. Ronald Duncan, the librettist for Benjamin Britten's opera *The Rape of Lucrece* (1947) introduces Christian commentators framing the action. Neither, however, tackles the problem raised, but not resolved, in Livy. Why did Lucretia have to die at all?

The apparent answer in Lucretia's final words ('hereafter no unchaste woman shall live through the example of Lucretia') is no answer at all. If Lucretia was, as her menfolk insist, innocent, why should she be regarded as setting a precedent for voluntary unchastity?

Saint Augustine stated the problem clearly. Most early Christian writers had no difficulty with the idea that loss of life was preferable even to involuntary loss of chastity. For Saint Augustine, however, the question of mental guilt or innocence was highly relevant; he refused to condemn the decision of the nuns who had chosen not to commit suicide after their rape by the Goths who sacked Rome in AD 410. He discusses Lucretia's story at length in *The City of God*, and reaches a dilemma. If Lucretia's mind consented to the rape, she was adulterous, and her death was the execution of justice; if her mind was innocent, then her death was suicide and sinful. 'If she was made an adulteress, why is she praised? If she was chaste, why was she killed?'

Rape and politics

The answer lies, from a Roman point of view, not in debate about Lucretia's guilt or innocence, but in the political aspect of the story. For the Romans, Lucretia's rape and death, like the peril and death of Verginia, are incidents within larger, political, narratives which are about the world of men.

For Livy and his contemporaries the stories had a special relevance; they saw the uncontrolled passions and desires of men who put themselves before the state as both the symptoms and the causes of the troubles of the late Republic, which ended in the collapse of what they thought of as democratic government. These had to be brought back under control; part of the programme of Augustus for mending the torn fabric of Roman society was the introduction of new and severe laws which made adultery a criminal offence, carrying severe penalties. That was the sort of lesson to be drawn from the tyrannical behaviour of Appius, and of Tarquinius and his son, and its consequences.

The women Lucretia and Verginia were the triggers for the lust of the tyrannical males Tarquin and Appius. Assault on them violated the autonomous control exercised by a husband or father within his own family, and set a bad precedent. (This was a principle recognised also in the Roman law of damages; insult or injury to a woman, or injury to a slave, was treated as damaging to the father, husband or owner.) The deaths of Lucretia, who is now 'damaged goods', and of Verginia, who seems about to be made so by force, reject any notion that such assaults may ever be regarded as tolerable, and so they preserve order and mutual respect among Roman men. The public parade of the corpses also provides the necessary provocation for the rest of the men of the community to unite against the tyrant who threatens their liberties.

Some gods old and new

As we have seen the major gods in the Roman pantheon were assimilated to or equated with the great Olympian gods of the Greeks, and their genealogies and the stories told about them by Roman writers were those told about their Olympian originals. Several foreign gods were also introduced to Rome, without being given Roman equivalents. Then there were the Romans' own lesser gods, honoured by the Romans, privately and also publicly, with shrines, offerings and rituals, but with few stories told about them, and sometimes not even any clear idea of their nature and identity.

To run through even the names of all the Roman gods would be tedious, but an example will give some idea of how little the Romans themselves could tell about them.

A forgotten god: who was Vediovis?

Vediovis (also sometimes called Veiovis or Vedius) had three festivals marked in the Roman calendar, on 1 January, 7 March and 21 May, and two temples at Rome. The first two festivals are the anniversaries, respectively, of the dedication in 194 and 192 BC of the two temples. There had been an earlier temple on the Capitol site; votive deposits from the seventh century BC have been found. Varro said that the Sabine king Titus Tatius introduced Vediovis to Rome; Ovid had the idea that the temple was in the place where Romulus set up his sanctuary. Livy thought both temples were dedicated to Jupiter.

Who was Vediovis and where did his name originate? Ovid says confidently: 'He is Jupiter when young [*iuvenis*]'. Beside his statue was an image of a she-goat; when Jupiter was an infant, the nymphs on Crete fed him with goat's milk. As for the name, 'Spelt [a kind of grain] that has not grown properly countrymen call *vegrandia*, and anything little they call *vesca*. So if that is the meaning, then may I not suspect that Vediovis is little Jove?'

In the second century AD a lawyer called Aulus Gellius published his *Noctes Atticae*, twenty volumes of little essays on a variety of topics (nowadays, he might have had a regular column on the features page of *The Times*). He tried hard to explain Vediovis. Jove and Diovis, he said, were given their names from helping (*iuvando*), and the prefix *ve-* sometimes negatived a word, so Vediovis was 'Anti-Jove', a god who did harm. Alternatively, because the statue in the shrine on the Capitol held arrows, obviously meant to do harm, many said that Vediovis was Apollo. Clearly, Gellius knew no more than anyone else.

Relief from a sarcophagus showing images of the Dioscuri and Jupiter being carried in a covered wagon, probably in a religious procession.

A few of the 'immigrant' gods have stories attached to them, usually in connection with the introduction of their worship to Rome. Here are two examples.

The Dioscuri

According to the Greeks, 'Zeus's boys' (*Dios kouroi*), Castor and Polydeuces (Pollux to the Romans), who were specially honoured at Sparta, were the brothers of Helen of Troy. Their mother was a mortal woman, Leda. Zeus, who disguised himself as a swan to seduce her, was the father of Pollux, but his twin Castor was the son of Leda's husband Tyndareus, and was mortal. However, since Pollux refused the immortality to which his parentage entitled him unless Castor could share it, Zeus allowed a compromise, by which they spent alternate days in the underworld and up above. They protected mariners at sea (and are often shown with stars on their caps), and rode on white horses.

In 499 or 496 BC the Romans fought a great battle at Lake Regillus, near Tusculum, and defeated the Latins. During the battle, two young men riding white horses appeared on the Roman side. Immediately after the fighting, they appeared again in the Roman Forum, their horses bathed in sweat, and announced the Roman victory. They watered their horses in a pool sacred to the nymph Juturna (Virgil made her Turnus' sister), then vanished. Manifestation in battle was something the Dioscuri did; the Greeks knew of one or two instances in their own history.

More than three hundred years after Lake Regillus, in 168 BC, a man called Publius Vatinius was heading for Rome late one night when two handsome young men on white horses appeared to him and announced that the Roman commander Lucius Aemilius Paullus had just defeated Perseus, king of Macedon. He reported this to the Senate, but they thought that he was playing a practical joke, and imprisoned him for contempt of their dignity. Eventually a dispatch arrived from Paullus, announcing his victory at the battle of Pydna, and Vatinius was set free and given some land as a reward. The divine visitors were said to have watered their horses at the sacred pool on that occasion too; at any rate, the adjacent temple was unaccountably open.

This temple was in fact dedicated only to Castor (it had been vowed by the Roman commander during the battle of Lake Regillus). The Romans made more of Castor, the horseman, than Pollux, the boxer; sometimes they even spoke of them as 'the Castores'. In 304 BC an annual cavalry parade was instituted in Rome on 15 July, their festival; in census years (every five years or so) it was combined with a review of membership of the state cavalry. This parade eventually lapsed, but Augustus revived it, and celebrated it with great splendour. The state cavalry paraded, sometimes to the number of five thousand, in formal robes, crowned with laurel and wearing all their military decorations, starting at Mars' temple outside the city boundary and ending at the Forum.

The Romans had in fact taken over two gods who were already established among the Latins. A bronze plaque from Lavinium, dating to the sixth or fifth century BC, has a dedication apparently transliterated from Greek, 'To the *kouroi* Castor and Pollux.' There was a spring of Juturna at Lavinium and a temple of the Dioscuri nearby at Ardea. Some identified them with the Great Gods, the Di Penates ('household protectors'), originally brought from Samothrace to Troy, and thence to Italy by Aeneas.

When Ascanius was building Alba Longa, a strange thing happened. A special temple was built in Alba for the images of the two gods, and they were brought from Lavinium to their new home. During the night, however, they disappeared, although the temple doors were shut fast, and no damage was found either to the roof or to the walls of the enclosure. In due course they were found, standing on their old pedestals in Lavinium. They were brought back to Alba, with prayers and special propitiatory sacrifices, but the same thing happened again. In the end it was decided to let them stay in Lavinium and to send some men back there from Alba to take care of them. In historical times Roman magistrates went every year to Lavinium, to sacrifice to the Penates and to Vesta; it was at Rome itself, however, in the temple of Vesta, or so they believed, that the original Penates were now kept, along with the Palladium, a sacred image of Pallas Athena, brought by Aeneas himself from Troy, which was the Luck of the Roman People.

Castor and Pollux and another immigrant, Hercules, became literally household names among the Romans, who used their names in mild oaths – but, curiously, in a gender-specific way. Women, but not usually men, said *mecastor*; both men and women said *edepol*, but women were not supposed to say *mehercle* – perhaps because they were not allowed to share in the food sacrificed to Hercules at the Ara Maxima ('greatest altar').

Hercules and Cacus

The Ara Maxima stood in the Forum Boarium (Cattle Market) at Rome and was the centre for a special cult of Hercules. It is uncertain whether he became popular with merchants because of this location, or whether, as some think, he was there because he was introduced to Rome by Phoenician traders, being identified with their god Melkart, and already worshipped by merchants because of his own journeyings, and his reputation as 'the warder-off of ills'. At any rate, the Romans had their own story to account for the cult. Their Hercules has some of the personal qualities of his Greek original. He is not only a saviour of mankind from terrible monsters, but, it is hinted, a muscleman, rather greedy and not too bright, with a quick temper.

On his return from the far West after his tenth Labour, Hercules came to the Tiber, driving the cattle which he had taken from the three-bodied monster Geryon. He paused to rest in a grassy meadow by the river. Heavy with food and drink, he dropped off to sleep, and a local shepherd, a strong, fierce man called Cacus, stole the finest of the cattle. To confuse the trail, he dragged them away backwards by their tails and hid them in a cave. Hercules was totally baffled, seeing only tracks leading away from the cave, and began to drive off the rest of the herd. Some of them began to low, and were answered by those in the cave. The trick was exposed; Hercules went after Cacus and struck him dead with his club.

That was the 'straight' story, as told by Livy. In the *Aeneid* Virgil turned the tale into a lurid supernatural fantasy, which reads almost like the screenplay for the special effects department of a film studio. Virgil's Cacus was no human being, but a hideous, fire-breathing man-monster, offspring of Vulcan, who lived in a cavern. He ate human flesh. The ground around his cave on the Aventine hill stank with freshly-shed blood, and around the entrance hung rotting human heads. He was a coward; when Hercules came after him, he turned and fled into his cave, blocking the entrance by cutting a chain and dropping a huge rock, originally installed by his father Vulcan, so that it jammed immovably between the doorposts. Hercules strained, but could not shift it, nor could he find another entrance. Finally he climbed higher up the hill and pulled up by its roots the great rock that formed the roof of the cave; thunder crashed, the earth shook and the river ran backward. Daylight poured into the foul den, showing Cacus cowering in a corner, howling. Hercules hurled down on him every missile he could lay his hands on, but Cacus spewed out great billows of thick black smoke, shot with flames, and so hid himself. Hercules leaped down into the thick of the smoke and fire, laid hold of Cacus and, literally, tied him in a knot, then strangled him until his eyes started from his head. He burst open the entrance, and hauled out the corpse.

After the death of Cacus, the local people, led by Evander, in gratitude to Hercules for ridding them of their oppressor, instituted a ritual in his honour. Every year on 12 August oxen were sacrificed and there was a feast. The cult was

A cavalry procession, led by musicians towards a shrine where sacrifice is being made: a relief from a cinerary urn (c. 100 BC).

administered by two Roman families, the Potitii and the Pinarii. The Pinarii arrived late for the first feast, and missed their share of the entrails; and so they were never ever served with that portion of the sacrifice. In 312 BC the cult was taken over by the state (Livy hints at some underhand doings). The Appius Claudius (later known as 'the Blind') who was censor in that year authorised the Potitii to instruct public slaves in the ritual, in order to hand it over to them. Within a year all the Potitii were dead, and their clan and name extinct, and a few years later Claudius went blind. (The Potitii in fact are not otherwise heard of in history, though some Pinarii survived into later times.)

The ritual had some peculiar features. No woman was allowed to share in the sacrificial meat. No other gods must be invoked. Dogs were excluded from the precinct. Plutarch had his ideas about the reasons. Other gods were not mentioned, because Hercules was merely a demigod. Hercules could not abide dogs, because of all the trouble he had been given by Cerberus, the three-headed dog guarding Hell, and because the battle in which his twin brother was killed arose because of a quarrel about a dog. Women were excluded because Carmenta (see p. 20) arrived late.

Propertius, in mock-epic style, gives a different explanation. Killing Cacus was thirsty work, and when Hercules asked to be allowed to drink at a spring in a shrine sacred to the Good Goddess (whose rites were secret and reserved to women), the priestess refused him entrance. So Hercules smashed down the door and had his drink. Then he got his own back; he told the priestess that he was setting up an altar of his own, as a thank-offering for recovering his cattle, but no women would be allowed to join in *his* rites.

Cacus and Cacu

There was another version of the story, found in Roman authors at least as early as the second century BC. The cattle belonged to a Greek shepherd called Recaranus, or Garanus, who was called 'a Hercules' because of his size and strength. His cattle were stolen by Cacus, who was Evander's slave. Evander found out, returned the cattle, and handed Cacus over for punishment.

Is this just a rationalised version of the Hercules story or, as some think, a separate, Italian story which has blended with it? To add to the confusion, 'Recaranus' and 'Garanus' both look like garbled forms of Geryon – but Hercules, not Cacus the slave, stole his cattle. Anyway, Cacus, it has been pointed out, is the Greek word for 'bad' (*kakos*), and Evander means, literally 'Goodman'. Calling the thief Cacus also helped the Romans to explain the name of a flight of steps leading up from the Forum Boarium to the Palatine.

However, that does not exhaust the stories about Cacus. Gnaeus Gellius, a Roman annalist (second century BC), said Cacus inhabited a place near the Tiber. King Marsyas had sent him as an envoy, accompanied by Megales the Phrygian, to King Tarchon the Etruscan, who imprisoned him. He escaped and went back where he had come from. Then he returned with reinforcements and seized the area around Vulturnus and Campania. When he dared to attempt to seize also those places which had been ceded to the Arcadians (i.e. Evander and his people), he was killed by Hercules, who happened to be there. Megales went to the Sabines and taught them the art of augury.

King Tarchon, who was the son or grandson of Hercules, was the founder of Etruscan Tarquinii, and knew the art of divination. One day a peasant was ploughing at Tarquinii, when out of the furrow emerged a being with grey hair and the face of a child. His name was Tages, and he proceeded to reveal to Tarchon and to the leaders of all the other Etruscan cities the art of divination from birds and from the entrails of animals. Marsyas, in Greek myth, was a satyr, and wind instrumentalist, who challenged Apollo (who played the harp) to a musical contest and lost; he was flayed for his pains. Gellius calls him a king of the Lydians, who founded a city on Lake Fucinus. There was an ancient belief that the Etruscans had come to Italy from Lydia.

This story is set in the mythological period before the foundation of Rome, but it might just contain the germ of an account of historical relations between Etruscan rulers in different parts of Italy in the sixth century BC; before then, Etruscans had spread both north and south, establishing colonies in northern Italy and as far south as Campania.

'Cacu' is well documented in Etruscan iconography. He appears, with a companion 'Artile', on a fourth-century BC bronze mirror, being ambushed by two warriors, and as their prisoner in relief carvings on no fewer than eight alabaster funerary urns, from the second century BC. This Cacus is no monster, nor even a hulking shepherd, but a handsome young man, evidently a seer and diviner. He is playing a lyre and Artile, perhaps his assistant, holds a diptych with some writing. The men ambushing him – perhaps hoping to benefit from the inside knowledge which his skills can provide – are no other than Caelius and Aulus Vibenna, whom we have already met (see p. 40). History and myth are mingling again.

How the Etruscan Cacu the seer was gradually metamorphosed into the Roman Cacus the monster – and the particular reasons why the Romans at various periods wanted to change the angle of the stories – has been the object of much modern discussion and speculation. This much appears clear: once more, we seem to have caught the Romans 'editing out' an alternative, Etruscan, history of central Italy.

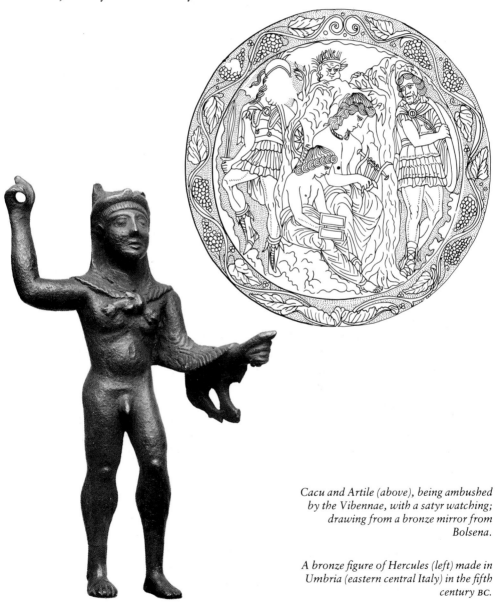

Cacu and Artile (above), being ambushed by the Vibennae, with a satyr watching; drawing from a bronze mirror from Bolsena.

A bronze figure of Hercules (left) made in Umbria (eastern central Italy) in the fifth century BC.

*A Lar (right), holding a
drinking-horn and a libation dish.*

*A handle of a silver patera (below):
beneath a figure of Fortune is a
country shrine, and at the foot a
woman sacrificing at an altar.*

Cults and festivals

The Romans celebrated many religious cults, both privately and publicly. In the country, farmers sacrificed to the appropriate gods before each job of work. The elder Cato, in the early second century BC, gives details in his farming manual of a number of their rituals; two hundred years later, when a romantic poet, Albius Tibullus, fantasises about living a rural idyll with his mistress playing the farmer's wife, he imagines her making little offerings of grapes or corn-ears, or libations of wine. Roman houses had a shrine at which daily offerings were made before figures of the Genius (protecting spirit) of the head of household, and of the Penates (gods of the store-cupboard), and the Lares. There were also public Lares (Lares Compitales) in the countryside and in towns, guarding crossroads where land-holdings or town districts adjoined. Their festivals were the occasion for jolly neighbourhood parties, and the emperor Augustus exploited their community function by linking their worship to that of the Genius of the emperor. Neither public Lares nor those of the household have individual names or histories.

Dozens of public religious occasions are listed in the Roman calendar, though we have details about what happened on only a few. Here are three of the most colourful.

Anna Perenna: a Roman Hogmanay

The Ides of March (15th), the day when Julius Caesar was assassinated in 44 BC, was the festival of Anna Perenna. Until about 153 BC the year began on 1 March, so the Ides fell about the time of the first full moon of the new year. On the previous day, the 14th, according to a late Roman writer, a man dressed in skins was beaten with rods and chased out of the city (exactly the same thing used to be done, on New Year's Eve, in farms on the island of Lewis).

The name Anna Perenna suggests that she was a personification of the yearly cycle; she was envisaged as an old woman. Ovid, typically, offers a number of explanations. One, perhaps his own invention, is that she was Dido's sister. After Dido's death, Carthage was invaded by local people and Anna fled by boat, arriving eventually in Latium. Aeneas met her and brought her to his palace; but his wife Lavinia was jealous and plotted her death. Warned by Dido in a dream, Anna fled and was carried off by the river Numicus. Those searching for her heard a voice from the water, saying that she was now a nymph. 'In an ever-flowing river (*amne perenne*) I hide, and Anna Perenna I am called.'

One of the Penates, with a cornucopia and a libation dish.

Wine, women and dance at a festival: a painting from a tomb in Rome.

But Ovid thinks more likely the story that, during the first Secession of the Plebs, the people who had gone to the Sacred Mount began to run out of food. There was an old woman called Anna, born outside the city at Bovillae, who was poor but industrious. With her trembling old hands she baked loaves of country bread, and every morning she brought them, piping hot, and distributed them among the people. Later they set up a statue of her, in gratitude.

Her festival was held at the first milestone along the Via Flaminia, to the north of Rome. People brought picnics and sat on the grass. Some brought tents, others built shelters of branches of reeds. They drank wine, praying for as many years as they drank cups – so, naturally, they tried to drink as many as possible. Then they would begin to sing popular songs, picked up in the theatres, and to dance. Eventually, they reeled off home, all drunk together.

Ovid adds that girls chanted ribald verses, and he explains why: they commemorated a trick played by Anna. Just after she became a goddess, Mars came to her one day for help. He had fallen in love, he said, with Minerva, and wanted to marry her (other authors say it was a goddess called Nerio who became Mars' wife). Anna kept fobbing him off, but eventually said that Minerva had agreed. Mars went home and got the bridal chamber ready, and the bride was escorted to him, with a veil on her face – but turned out to be Anna.

Nonae Caprotinae: the Feast of Slave-Women

This was held on the Nones (7th) of July, and was also a picnic day. The story about its origin is almost the Rape of the Sabines turned inside out.

Soon after 390 BC Roman territory was attacked by the Latins. They sent to Rome demanding that the Romans give them free-born virgins for marriage. The Romans were just recovering from the sack of the city by the Gauls, and wanted to avoid war so were reluctant to refuse, but they were worried that the 'brides' were really intended only as hostages. A slave girl called Tutula or, some say, Philotis, told the magistrates what to do. They picked out the prettiest and most aristocratic-looking slave women, dressed them like free-born brides, complete with gold jewellery, and sent them with Tutula (or Philotis) to the Latin camp near the city.

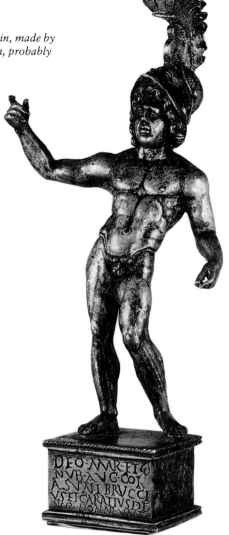

A statue of Mars from Britain, made by Gaulish or British craftsmen, probably after an Italian original.

Pretending it was a festival day for Romans, the slave women got the Latins drunk, and during the night they took away their swords, while Tutula sent the magistrates the secret signal on which they had agreed. She climbed a tall wild fig-tree and held up a lighted torch, spreading cloths behind it to conceal the light from the Latins. The magistrates urgently called out the soldiers, who tumbled out of the city and, not knowing what was going on, shouted each others' names in their confusion. They stormed the camp of the Latins while they were still asleep, and killed most of them.

All this, says Plutarch, was commemorated in the festival. Crowds of slave girls, gaily dressed (probably in their mistresses' clothes), ran out of the city gate, shouting common male personal names, like 'Gaius', 'Marcus', 'Lucius' and so on. They joked with all the men they met. Then they had playful fights with each other – a mock battle. After that, they sat and feasted under shelters made from fig-tree branches.

Varro says that the Nones were called *Caprotinae* because women in Latium sacrificed on that day to Juno Caprotina under a wild fig-tree (*caprificus*), offering her fig-juice instead of milk, and using a stick from the tree in the ritual (perhaps to hit each other in the mock fighting), and a later author adds that both slave women and free took part. The festival may have been a sort of female version of the Saturnalia in December, when masters waited on their slaves – useful as a safety valve, in maintaining social order. During the early Empire, masters left that part of the celebrations to their children; probably the mistresses stopped taking part in the Caprotine Nones as well.

The religious purpose for the festival may have been to promote fertility, in women as well as agriculture (the agricultural writer Columella recommended pollinating fig-trees in July). In the Latin town of Lanuvium at the beginning of February there was a festival of Juno Sospita ('Protectress'), who is shown wearing the skin of a goat (*caper* or *capra* according to gender) on her head. Young girls, blindfolded, entered her sacred grove with offerings of barley cakes for a sacred snake. If it ate the cakes, the girls were proved to be virgins, and the year would be fertile.

Goat or fig-tree? Plutarch has another story. There was a Roman festival called *Poplifugia* (flight of the people). No one knew what it was supposed to be commemorating; one idea was that it originated at the disappearance of Romulus, which happened near a place called Goat's Marsh. 'They go out of the city and sacrifice at the Goat's Marsh (for *capra* is their word for she-goat); and as they go out to the sacrifice they shout out native [i.e. Roman] names, like Marcus, Lucius, Gaius, imitating the way in which, on the day when Romulus vanished, they shouted to each other in alarm and confusion.' Unfortunately, Plutarch the Greek is confused, thinking that the Poplifugia (which was on 5 July) and the Nonae Caprotinae fell on the same day. The Nones in the Roman calendar were on the fifth day of the month *except* in March, May, July and October, when they were on the seventh.

Lupercalia: beating the bounds?

The festival of the Lupercalia on 15 February is easier to describe than to explain. Two colleges of priests took part, the Luperci Quintilii and Fabii; a third, the Julii, named after Julius Caesar, was instituted in 45 BC but did not continue long after his death.

Proceedings started at the Lupercal cave at the south-west corner of the Palatine hill. Animals were sacrificed, goats and, unusually, a dog, and cakes prepared by the Vestal Virgins with flour made from the first ears of the previous year's harvest. The blood on the blade of the sacrificial knife was smeared on the foreheads of two of the Luperci, and wiped off with a piece of wool soaked in milk; then the young men had to laugh. The goatskins were cut into strips. Some of them the young men girt round themselves, then, naked except for these girdles, the teams ran in different directions, originally all around the Palatine hill (later this seems to have been altered to a partial circuit, and a sprint up and down the Sacred Way in the Forum) and back to the Lupercal. On the way they struck at bystanders, especially women, with goatskin thongs.

By Augustus' time, the fun may have been getting slightly out of hand. Livy talked of the original celebrants' playful and frolicsome antics – which Valerius Maximus later took to mean that they had too much to drink. Augustus ordered that only youths old enough to have a beard were to be allowed to run. Nevertheless, the festival survived until AD 494 when Pope Gelasius I claimed it for the Church, as the Feast of Purification of the Virgin Mary.

The sacrificed dog was a puzzle. Plutarch, as usual full of ideas, had four suggestions: first, the Greeks used dogs as purificatory sacrifices, and also, in expiation, to Hecate, goddess of the underworld; second, Lupercalia was associated with wolves, and dogs were wolves' enemies; third, the Luperci were harassed by barking dogs as they ran; fourth, Pan approved of dogs, who guarded the flocks.

The antiquarian Varro interpreted the striking with thongs as a purification rite, but Ovid preferred what was probably the popular view, that it encouraged fertility; Plutarch gives both explanations. Shakespeare, in his *Julius Caesar*, picks up this detail. At the Lupercalia he has Caesar instruct his childless wife to stand in Mark Antony's way, to be struck. The most famous celebration of the festival was that of 44 BC, when Mark Antony, head of the Julian Luperci, publicly offered Julius Caesar a royal crown, which he refused three times. The occasion was probably chosen because of the crowds of spectators that gathered. This stage-managed demonstration that he had no regal ambitions did Caesar no good; one month later, he was assassinated.

Evander was supposed to have instituted a festival in honour of Pan Lycaeus, who was identified with the woodland god Faunus or with 'Inuus'. As far as aetiological explanations were wanted, the Romans believed that the Lupercalia in some way celebrated the origin of Rome (it was not the city's 'official birthday' – that came later, on 21 April). The route of the running was thought by some to be the boundary of the original Rome established by Romulus around the Palatine, starting and ending at his old nursery, the wolf's lair. The two teams were associated with Romulus and Remus. Ovid explains that once, when they were shepherd youths, while the goats sacrificed to Faunus were being cooked, a warning came that robbers were stealing the cattle. Romulus and Remus, each with a group of young men, chased off after them in different directions. Remus and his Fabii got back first with the rescued cattle, and ate up all the feast. In Christian times the race up and down the Sacred Way was ingeniously reinterpreted as representing sinful mankind running up and down hill to escape the Flood.

Such explanations, however, left a lot of details unaccounted for. Why the smearing with blood, the milk-soaked wool, and the laugh? Why the goatskin girdles and thongs? According to Plutarch, a Greek poet in the first century BC said that the blood commemorated the danger in which Amulius had placed the infants, and the milk their nourishment by the wolf. The goatskin thongs were sometimes explained as part of a purification rite (Varro, Plutarch).

A coin of 65 BC. (obverse): Juno Sospita in a goatskin headdress; (reverse) a woman offering something to an upraised serpent.

Ovid, interestingly, associates them with Juno, both as a goddess of fertility in women, and one who looks after women in childbirth, Juno Lucina, who had a temple on the Esquiline (Juno Sospita, the one with the goatskin cloak, was also worshipped at Rome, but elsewhere). Brides who want to be mothers, Ovid says, should allow themselves to be struck at the Lupercalia. Once upon a time, when Romulus was king, the birth-rate was disastrously low. 'What good did it do me,' cried Romulus, 'to have carried off the Sabine women?' There was a grove on the Esquiline, sacred to Juno. The women and their husbands went there and prayed to the goddess. Then the tops of the trees began to toss, and the voice of the goddess came from the grove: 'Let the sacred he-goat go in to [*inito* – which perhaps explains the name Inuus] Italian matrons.' The people were dumbstruck, not understanding. Then an augur, an Etruscan exile (but his name is long forgotten) killed a goat, and told the women to offer themselves to be struck with the hide, cut in strips. In the tenth month, the Romans became parents.

With the Lupercalia, one suspects, we have an example of a phenomenon dear to the hearts of students of mythology, a festival with a multiplicity of functions, which may have accumulated around one date in the calendar as a result of a long historical development. February (whose name Romans connected with purification) was the last month of the old year, a month of cleansings, purifications and preparation for new beginnings. Juno Sospita's day was the first. From the 13th to the 21st was the festival of the dead (*Parentalia*), when all temples were closed and family tombs were visited, followed on the 22nd by Loving Family day (*Caristia*). On the 27th the city bounds were walked in procession and there was a sacrifice. In March the new year began, and the new campaigning year for Rome's warriors.

The Lupercalia is integrated into the sequence of the Roman religious year. It was a festival of purification for the community, but also, it has recently been suggested, it functioned both as a fertility ritual for women and a rite of passage for young men, by symbolic re-enactment of birth and the aftermath, up to and including the time when babies, once out of the post-natal danger period, start to respond interactively – which would account for the blood, the milk, the laugh, and the association with the infant Romulus and Remus.

That may be so. For the Romans, it was an interesting day's fun, at a dreary time of year, and they had their own stories to account for it.

Conclusion

Roman myths and legends served a variety of purposes, and so their details were not sacrosanct; they were changed, embellished and adapted at need. Some, as we have just seen, were stories to explain the rituals of festivals or to 'domesticate' foreign gods introduced to Rome. Others celebrated the patriotic and moral values cherished, at least as ideals, as being particularly Roman, while often at the same time offering explanations for historical events, or staking a noble family's claim to a prominent place in Rome's tradition. Central, and most important, were the legends about Rome's origins and early growth. These asserted Rome's claim to have been, from the first, outstanding and undefeated among the peoples of Italy (despite the alternative versions – fairly successfully suppressed – of other peoples), whom they were destined to rule. They also claimed for the Romans a share in the cultural birthright of the Greek civilisation they had conquered. More than all this, and despite their adaptation to bolster the power of the ruler under the imperial régime, they depicted Rome itself and its people as marked out by the gods to be the destined rulers of the whole world.

John 'Warwick' Smith, View of Rome. *Watercolour, 1780. In the centre is the Colosseum, with the Arch of Constantine on the left.*

Suggestions for further reading

There was room above to give only a limited number of the legends familiar to the Romans, and those for the most part briefly. It is possible to enjoy the more elaborate, and often vivid, accounts of Greek and Roman writers through English translations. Many of the works mentioned in the text are available in Penguin Classics, whose translations, several produced within the last few years, are lively and readable. Almost all the authors cited are published in the Loeb Classical Library; the translations used in that series were often written some time ago, and appear rather old-fashioned in consequence, but they have the added advantage, for those with some knowledge of Latin or Greek, of having a parallel text in the original language.

There are a number of modern books which can enhance appreciation and understanding of Roman legends and their nature. A collection of essays on a variety of topics, including several of the legends told in the present book, is contained in *Roman Myth and Mythology* (London, 1987) by J. N. Bremmer and N. M. Horsfall, two contrasting scholars, one of whom is mainly concerned with analysing the stories to trace the development of the traditions, the other with such matters as comparative mythology, and the relation between myth and ritual. H. H. Scullard, *Festivals and Ceremonies of the Roman Republic* (London, 1981) proceeds day by day through the religious calendar of a Roman year, with descriptions of many festivals and ceremonies, and the stories told to account for them.

For the relationship between myth and history, Michael Grant, *Roman Myths* (London, original publication 1971, recently reprinted) is a readable account of the ways in which these stories were manipulated or, in some cases, invented, in successive periods of Roman history to fulfil the purposes of members of the governing élite. T. P. Wiseman, *Clio's Cosmetics* (Leicester, 1979) discusses the concept of history among Roman historical writers, particularly in the first century BC, and their view of what we would call legend. For what is now thought to be known about the actual history of early Rome, see *The Cambridge Ancient History* (second edition), Volume VII, Part 2, 'The Rise of Rome to 220 BC' (1989), edited by F. W. Walbank and others.

The use of traditional myth in propaganda, and creation of a new personal myth by Julius Caesar, is discussed in *Divus Julius* (Oxford, 1971), by S. Weinstock. Study of similar propaganda for Rome's first emperor, Augustus, has produced much important recent work, of which readers are likely to find most interesting and accessible the discussion of the use of visual means of communication in P. Zanker, *The Power of Images in the Age of Augustus*, translated by A. Shapiro (Ann Arbor, Michigan, 1988); see also Susan Walker and Andrew Burnett, *The Image of Augustus* (London, 1981). The use of legends in visual propaganda (this time mainly under the Republic), and especially in coins, is also the subject of J. DeRose Evans: *The Art of Persuasion: political propaganda from Aeneas to Brutus* (Princeton, 1992).

Special mention should be made of I. Donaldson, *The Rapes of Lucretia: a Myth and its Transformations* (Oxford, 1982). The ideas of the Poet Laureate, Ted Hughes, on Shakespeare's version are to be found in his *Shakespeare and the Goddess of Complete Being* (London, 1992).

Index